W9-DAP-647

RENAISSANCE
LITERARY THEORY
AND PRACTICE

RENAISSANCE LITERARY THEORY AND PRACTICE

✣

Classicism in the Rhetoric and Poetic
Of Italy, France, and England
1400-1600

By

CHARLES SEARS BALDWIN

Edited with Introduction by
DONALD LEMEN CLARK

GLOUCESTER, MASS.
PETER SMITH
1959

BEATO THOMAE MORO
JVDICI
CVI STILVM ANGLICVM
LATINE REGENTI
PERSTABAT IN REGIA
QVAESTIONE PAX ROMANA

INTRODUCTION

W HEN he died in 1936 Charles Sears Baldwin, Professor of Rhetoric and English Composition at Columbia University, left the unpublished manuscript which here appears in print. At the request of his family, I undertook to prepare the manuscript for publication and see it through the press. As a devoted student, colleague, and friend I have been happy to do so.

Baldwin's *Renaissance Literary Theory and Practice* takes its place as the continuation of his previously published studies: *Ancient Rhetoric and Poetic* (1924) and *Medieval Rhetoric and Poetic* (1928), both published by the Macmillan Company. It takes up the story where *Medieval Rhetoric and Poetic* left off in 1400 and carries it on to 1600.

The first sentences of his preface to the first study suggest that Baldwin had the present study in mind before 1924. "To interpret ancient rhetoric and poetic afresh from typical theory and practice is the first step toward interpreting those traditions of criticism which were most influential in the Middle Age. Medieval rhetoric and poetic, in turn, prepare for a clearer comprehension of the Renaissance renewal of allegiance to antiquity."

Like the two earlier studies, it is firmly based on the Aristotelian philosophy of composition embodied in the *Rhetoric* and the *Poetic*. Baldwin adheres to the sound rhetoric which aims at enhancing the subject and repudiates the sophistic rhetoric which aims at enhancing the speaker. Rhetoric and poetic are different in aim and different in their modes of composition. Consequently he considers poetic deviated when it becomes confused with rhetoric and perverted when controlled by sophistic.

Had he lived, Baldwin would have written more than here appears. He had planned a chapter on Renaissance education which would have demonstrated more fully the channels through which poetical theory reached poetical practice. In the chapter "Sixteenth Century Poetics" he had planned sections on Castelvetro and Sibillet which were never written. Other writers on literary theory he deliberately omitted as less typical, less significant, or less influential than the writers he discusses. His method was to go directly to the original sources, both for theory and for practice, to make his own translations, and to ignore secondary sources, which he rarely cites.

Although Chapters IV, V, VI, and VIII deal with literary forms: lyric, pastoral, romance, drama, tales, history, and essay, Baldwin was not attempting a history of Italian, French, and English literature in the fifteenth and sixteenth centuries. To have written such a history would have involved a completeness he never intended. He was assaying samples of literature for literary values. Especially was he tracing the influences of sound literary theory on sound literary practice, and the disastrous results in literature of the misapplication of rhetorical theory to poetic and the composition of story and drama. As literary critic and teacher of composition, he saw no good reason why modern literature, in theory or in practice, should make the same mistakes that were made in ancient times, the Middle Age, and the Renaissance. He believed that modern literature, modern criticism, and modern teaching should learn from the mistakes of others as well as from their own.

Before Baldwin's death I had read the manuscript in two states as I had the two earlier works. Further, the manuscript was read and criticized by Dr. Caroline Ruutz-Rees of Rosemary Hall and Professor William G. Crane of The College of the City of New York. To these friends, and to the others whose aid I have been unable to discover, the author's and the editor's gratitude is due. Professor Marshall Whithed Baldwin, son of Charles Sears Baldwin, read both the galley and the page proofs. My colleagues, Professors Harry Morgan Ayres and Nelson Glenn McCrea, advised on the proofs and other details. I join with the Baldwin estate in gratitude to the generous assistance of the officers and editorial staff of the Columbia University Press.

DONALD LEMEN CLARK

Columbia University
September, 1939

CONTENTS

CONTENTS

RENAISSANCE
LITERARY THEORY
AND PRACTICE

Chapter I

THE RENAISSANCE AS A
LITERARY PERIOD

THE word *renaissance* suggests a state of mind, the sense of recovering something neglected by one's literary ancestors. "Ours is a new day," says the fifteenth century. "We have escaped from the decadence of our fathers into the purer poetry. We have recovered the great tradition and are setting it forward." So the English eighteenth century, which had again repudiated "gothic night," was in turn repudiated in the manifesto of the *Lyrical Ballads* and scorned by Keats as "a schism nourished in foppery and barbarism." *The* Renaissance, then, is it only one such instance of self-consciousness among the many that mark so-called periods of literature? The fifteenth and sixteenth centuries were regarded not only at the time, but long and widely, as an actual new day, *the* Renaissance. Histories of literature, no less than those of politics and society, have treated it as a distinct period. Though more recent histories have found it less distinct, it still claims attention as a widespread cult of the ancient classics. Its leading ideas permeated western Europe; and its new day, though it was bent toward nationalism, was conceived but secondarily as national progress, primarily as a general reanimation from ancient ideals long neglected. Thus it is not only the most familiar example of a

typical recurrence in literary history; it remains the cardinal experience of classicism. Though we may no longer
speak of the fifteenth and sixteenth centuries as a reawak-
ening of literature equal to that of painting, we may still
speak of *the* Renaissance.

The common sixteenth-century view of accomplished
restoration after medieval decadence is expressed (1527)
by Guillaume Budé.

The best part, I think, we now have in our hands, saved from
the deluge of more than a thousand years; for a deluge indeed, calamitous to life, had so drained and absorbed literature
itself and the kindred arts worthy of the name, and kept them
so dismantled and buried in barbarian mud that it was a
wonder they could still exist (*De studio literarum,* 1527; Basel
ed. 1533).

In 1558 the sober Minturno is merely less certain as to
dates.

For who of you is unaware that from the time when the
Roman Empire, for all its power and eminence, began to totter
and lean, literature was asleep, not to say overwhelmed and
buried, till the time of Petrarch? From then on, it has been
so steadily regaining the light that now it has been almost
recalled from that [medieval] rude and barbarous teaching
to its ancient cult (*De poeta,* 1559, p. 14).

The *Poetica* (1561) of Julius Caesar Scaliger surprised
no one by bringing the history of Latin poetry to date
without even mentioning the Middle Age. He might
include his own poems; he need not include the medieval
hymns. Scorn of the Middle Age was a Renaissance literary commonplace. The history of literature has to be

rewritten from age to age, first to satisfy such prejudices, then to dispel them. The art that survives these reinterpretations, the books or the paintings that still compel admiration and study, are vindicated, whatever their period, as classics. Meantime the perception of these has been repeatedly obscured both by preoccupation with some idealized great period and by pride in one's own time.

What, then, has the longer perspective of history shown to be the literary progress of the Middle Age and the distinctive direction of the Renaissance? Two answers have been found in the fourteenth-century borderland: (1) the culmination of medieval development in the literary triumph of the vernaculars, and (2) the beginning of a new literary influence in the revival of Greek. Two more belong to the fifteenth century: (3) the vogue of that humanistic Latin which rejected the medieval freedom for conformity to the style of an idealized great period, and (4) the establishment of printing.

The literary triumph of the vernaculars is forecast in Dante. The supreme achievement of the *Divina Commedia* is eloquent at once of the Middle Age and of the literary future. The vogue of Boccaccio and the wider influence of Petrarch were not of their Latin, but of their vernacular writings. The traditional superiority of Latin, indeed, as the language of literature not only lingered; it was upheld by humanism; but the tradition had gradually to yield to the facts. The fourteenth century closed with the convincing achievement of Chaucer in English. To French also, though individual eminence was less, the century promised the literary future. The long medieval course of Latin had reached its term. The new literary day was for the new languages. None the less that new day was medieval, not merely in date, but in being the culmination of a medieval progress. The language of literature, medieval experience had learned, must be the language of communication. So it had long been in Latin; so it had become, within medieval conditions, in Tuscan, French, and English. No subsequent change through Greek, or humanistic Latin, or even printing, more affected the outlook and direction of literature than the medieval rise of the vernaculars from literary acceptance to literary eminence.

Greek, generally in abeyance through most of the Middle Age, was studied by both Petrarch and Boccaccio and had its professor at Florence in 1396. Its spread in the fifteenth century was stimulated both by the movement for the reunion of the "Greek" Church with Rome and by the influx of Greek scholars after the fall of Constantinople in 1453. But it never threatened the traditional eminence of Latin. Renaissance literary dialogues were less often Platonic in form than Ciceronian; and the direct influence of Theocritus on revived pastoral is hard to distinguish from the indirect influence through the *Bucolics* of Vergil. Still more important to remember is that Greek influence, direct or indirect, stopped short of Greek composition. Greek dramaturgy, perhaps the cardinal Greek influence on later times, remained ineffective in the Renaissance. The *Poetic* of Aristotle did not oust the "Ars poetica" of Horace. Slowly grasped, Greek dramaturgy hardly shaped plays before the seventeenth century. The sixteenth century was still repeating Horace and following Seneca or carrying on the experience of the miracle plays or learning by stage experiment. Nor was verse narrative, even when called epic, attentive to the Aristotelian doctrine of sequence. The integration of Tasso's *Jerusalem,* which found its model in the *Aeneid,* is quite exceptional. The manuscripts circulating in the fourteenth century and the early fifteenth, as well as the texts later printed, show as ready a welcome for the decadent Greek literature of Alexandria as for the great names of Athens. With Homer came in not only the *Anthology,* but even those "Greek romances" which are aggregations of melodrama. The Renaissance vogue of Plato involved from its beginning the cultivation of the neo-Platonists. On the other hand, Greek added to higher education a language experience that held its place for some three hundred years and was expected of all scholars.

Renaissance scorn of the Middle Age was not merely a general complacency; it was especially a repudiation of the freedom of medieval Latin. Latin style must conform to the habits of its great period; and this restoration was a prime object of Renaissance classicism. In 1472 Guillaume Fichet, scholar and rhetorician, wrote to another rhetorician, Robert Gaguin:

I feel the greatest satisfaction, most learned Robert, in the flourishing here at Paris, where they used to be unknown, of poetic compositions and all the parts of eloquence. For when in my youth I first left the Baux country to study at Paris the learning of Aristotle, I used to be much astonished at finding so rarely in all Paris an orator and a poet. No one was studying Cicero night and day as many do now. No one knew how to write verse correctly or to scan the verse of others. For the school of Paris, having lost the habit of Latinity, had hardly emerged from ignorance in the field of discourse. But from our days dates a better epoch; for the gods, to speak poetically, and the goddesses are reviving among us the art of speaking well.[1]

In 1476 Lorenzo Valla prefaced a manual widely current in the fifteenth and sixteenth centuries, *De elegantia linguae latinae*, with his shame at medieval Latin and his confidence in the restoration.

But as I would say more, I am choked and inflamed by grief, compelled to weep as I behold from what estate and to what estate eloquence has fallen. For what lover of letters or of the public weal could restrain his tears at seeing it debased as when Rome was captured by the Gauls: everything so over-turned, burned, dislocated that hardly survives even the very citadel? These many centuries not only has no one spoken Latin aright, but no one reading it has understood; the books of the ancients have not been grasped and are not grasped now; as if with the loss of the Roman Empire had been lost all pride in speaking and knowing Roman, and the splendor of Latinity, faded by mould and rust, were forgotten. . . . But the less happy were those former times which produced no single scholar, the more we may congratulate our own times, in which, if we but strive a little further, I am confident that not only the Roman city, but still more the Roman language, and with it all liberal studies, shall be restored.

The Middle Age, then, could not write Latin. Not John of Salisbury, not Dante, not even Aquinas was really

[1] In H. Chamard, *Les Origines de la poésie française de la Renaissance* (Paris, 1920), p. 256.

eruditus! Fifty years later the judicious Bembo reports the restoration as accomplished.

Latin has so far been purged of the rust of the untaught centuries that today it has regained its ancient splendor and charm.[2]

Renaissance classicism thus ignored the medieval Latin progress. This deliberate breaking with the past could not, indeed, stop the sun; but it did put back the hands of the clock. The humanistic cult of Augustan Latin as a literary norm widely affected all language study. Though its literary achievement has faded in the perspective of history, its literary experience has permanent significance.

The rapid diffusion of printing in the late fifteenth century was a change of so wide and deep consequence to literature as to become a revolution. The suddenly increased and rapidly increasing availability of books was by itself enough to make a renaissance. Further it gave their role to the great publishers: Aldus, Gryphius, the Juntas, Froben, the Étiennes, Plantin. But one of the first effects of printing was to prolong or widen the influence of books characteristically medieval: Boethius and Bede, Alain de Lille, Aquinas, Hugh of St Victor. With Geoffrey of Monmouth were printed such romances as *Mélusine* and *Pontus and the Fair Sidoine.* Even Merlin was resuscitated. Neither Ariosto for his Carolingians nor Spenser for his Arthurians needed manuscript sources. Moreover the presses answered continuing demand for the *Golden Legend* and for such typically medieval com-

[2] Bembo, *Prose,* II. xxi (Venice, 1525).

pends as that of Petrus Comestor, the *Speculum* of Vincent of Beauvais, and even the *Etymologiae* of Isidore. They brought out not only the greater Cicero, recovered in 1422, but also the elder Seneca, Lucan, Aulus Gellius, Statius, Ausonius, Claudian, Sidonius, the medieval favorites. They multiplied for schools Donatus and Priscian, Diomedes and Martianus Capella. The collection entitled *Auctores* (or *Actores*) *octo* set before boys the *De contemptu mundi*, the *Tobias* of Matthieu de Vendôme, an *Isopet* and *Cathonet,* and the *Proverbia* of Alain de Lille. The hackneyed *De inventione,* the *Rhetorica ad Herennium,* and the hardy perennial "Ars poetica" of Horace had new lease of life. Medieval courtly verse forms, especially the *balade,* though scorned by Du Bellay and Ronsard, persisted not only with Villon, but in the huge printed collection of 1501, *Le Jardin de plaisance.* One of the first effects of printing was to prolong the Middle Age.

If the recovery of Greek, then, and even the establishment of printing, did not upset historical continuity, what of the lapse of feudalism? The most picturesque scene of the fifteenth and sixteenth centuries was such a ducal court as that of Urbino, Mantua, or Ferrara. Its lavish splendor broke from the ruins of feudalism. It was a triumph of individual violence amid the dislocation of medieval loyalties. This type of court, established and maintained by such professional soldiers as Sir John Hawkwood, became in Elizabethan imaginations a proverb at once of magnificence and of ruthlessness. Macchiavelli's realistic statesmanship was interpreted as diabolic; and Italian dukes were staged with daggers and poison. Though this foreign prejudice and exaggeration were largely melodrama, the court poets themselves hint at actual ruthlessness in contrast to their idealized Carolingian chivalry. Boiardo made the romantic literary escape frankly; and even Ariosto felt its spell. So Sir Thomas Malory, who needed no lessons in violence from Italy, escapes from the bitter Wars of the Roses to Camelot. So a French professional soldier is idealized as the Chevalier Bayard. With feudal service already obsolete in the fourteenth century, chivalry had become altogether what it had always been in part, poetry. There, indeed, was a breach with the Middle Age; and it is earliest and clearest in Italy. The ducal court is distinct both from the idealized castle of the medieval romances and from the actual castle of the Middle Age.

Patrons of painters and architects, the ducal courts had also their orators and their poets. The orators had the more distinct function of furnishing on occasion ceremonious letters and addresses; they might be secretaries and sometimes librarians. The poets devised the characteristic Renaissance pageants for the solemn entries of distinguished visitors or triumphing dukes. Both were spokesmen in obituary, in nuptial greeting, in other encomium. The pervasive encomium of the Renaissance may have been directly stimulated by the ducal courts. How important they were as literary centers is more difficult to determine. Having a poet or an orator on the premises has not always constituted a literary center. In some cases the courts may have fostered literature less than they added it to their own adornment; in some cases a court poet might feel himself rather thwarted than stimulated. At least they were important enough to become literary fictions. The setting of one of the most characteristic and influential dialogues of the Renaissance, Castiglione's *Cortegiano* (1528) is the court of Urbino. Idealized of course, this fixed the type of gracious culture which offsets Macchiavelli's realism and the Elizabethan melodrama of lust and murder. The very name of the book has literary significance. No single word is more characteristic of Renaissance literature than *courtier.* In its wider sense it describes not only Ariosto and Tasso, but also Ronsard and Spenser.

The more permanent literary center of the period of rapid commercial expansion was first Florence, where the new commercial aristocracy lived cheek by jowl with the bourgeoisie; then Lyon, commercial for a thousand years, literary outpost of Italy in France. These are cardinal examples of the intellectual interests and achievements stirred in Venice, Bruges, London, and the other commercial cities, by trade and printing. In Medicean Florence social eminence demanded not only some interest in the arts, but some acquaintance with them. Nicolao Nicoli, merchant and scholar, was connoisseur enough to see at a glance that the chalcedony on a boy's neck was a "Policreto." The ideal of educated taste and skill set up by Castiglione for Urbino is no less clear among the merchant princes and their courtiers in Florence. The great Cosimo dei Medici commissions Vespasiano to make him a library worthy of his position, though he is daringly reminded that libraries should not be made to order. In Venice Minturno addresses the preface of his *De poeta* to Gabriel Vinea, "pride of commerce, delight of scholars" (*mercatorum decus ac deliciae literatorum*). Lyon had wealthy leisure for the same reason as Venice. Among the greater publishers of the sixteenth century were its Gryphius, Rouville, and De Tournes. Its large Italian population had been swelled by the exile ensuing upon the Pazzi conspiracy. It published the romances of Alamanni. Its most original author, Louise Labé, wrote some of her sonnets in Italian. Maurice Scève was the more typically a poet of his time in composing elaborate pageants for its solemn entries. His uncle Guillaume's house was meantime a resort of scholars; and there is abundant other evidence of lively and various literary interchange. The literary leadership of Italy, then, was maintained less by the ducal courts than by the commercial cities. There it had animated the genius of Boccaccio and of Chaucer. The later influence of Italy on Wiat, Surrey, and Spenser, its more diffused influence through France, seem less fruitful for the progress of literature than the end of the Italian Middle Age.

Tardy recognition of this Italian continuity has led some historians to include in the Renaissance not only Chaucer, but Petrarch and Boccaccio, and even to begin it with Dante. But this, though it rebukes the complacency of the fifteenth and sixteenth centuries, tends to obscure the generally received significance of both Middle Age and Renaissance. The terms are not outworn. The division that they still express, after much revision of dates, is of general literary habits. It is the change from the feudal society living by manuscripts and reading aloud, with Latin for an international language of communication existing beside the established vernacular, to the rapidly commercializing society living by printed books amid widening education and nationalist aspirations, with Latin specialized as the vernacular widens its circle of readers. The latter is the society of the fifteenth and sixteenth centuries.

The distinctive literary changes, indeed, were hardly attained before the sixteenth century. Though humanism as a theory was established in the fifteenth, the literary product of that century was generally feeble, as of a Middle Age gone to seed. Even the sixteenth century, conscious of revival, eager for standards, proud of learning, preoccupied with classicism, is more significant in its theorizing than in its achievement, in criticism and study than in literary advance. Whereas medieval poetry ranged far beyond medieval poetic, first in Dante and last in Chaucer, Renaissance poetry shows less advance in composition. It has no Dante, no Chaucer. The *novella* does not seize and carry forward the more intense narrative found in his various experiments by Boccaccio. The *Heptameron* of Marguerite de Navarre is narratively inferior to the *Decameron*. The chivalric romances show a departure rather in style than in method from medieval romance; and their literary history from Ariosto to Spenser is not in terms of narrative art. Spenser is but the more typical of the Renaissance in that his great achievement of verse and style suffices without onward movement. The narrative slowness of his pageantry, the descriptive dilation, descend through the Renaissance partly from revived Alexandrianism, partly from medieval patterns discarded by Chaucer. Renaissance poets are not often even concerned with such a problem of composition as Chaucer's reconceiving and recomposing of a long old story, lately retold with new life by Boccaccio, in his verse novel *Troilus and Criseyde*.

For all its confidence in a new day, Renaissance literary theory repeats some medieval commonplaces. The *arts poétiques* of the sixteenth century prolong the vogue of the "Ars poetica" of Horace. The old doctrine of poetic inspiration is renamed Platonic. The slighting of composition by medieval manuals is continued. Renaissance manuals are no less generally limited to style; for the old preoccupation is confirmed by the new insistence on style as an accomplishment and as conformity to standard. Thus the Renaissance long accepted tacitly the medieval confusion of poetic with rhetoric. Cicero's *De oratore* was found to have lessons for poetry; Bembo, even as Johannes de Gerlandia, transferred from oratory to poetry the conventional classification of the "three styles"; and Minturno's *De poeta* is by itself a complete identification of poetic with rhetoric. But Renaissance theory gradually advanced. The successive reinterpretations of Aristotle's *Poetic* finally opened the way for seventeenth-century French classical drama. The better Renaissance rhetorics, using Quintilian as well as the greater Cicero to guide the increasing range and control of sixteenth-century prose, set forth a sounder and more fruitful classicism. Wherein classicism is typically a hindrance to literary progress, and wherein it is stimulus and guide, is amply revealed by the literary experience of the Renaissance.

Chapter II

LATIN, GREEK, AND THE VERNACULARS

I. HUMANISTIC LATIN

THE Middle Age had developed Latin style freely as a medium of communication and variously as a medium of expression. On these terms Latin had had a progressive history as the literary language of western Europe. Latin remained the literary language for Erasmus and More in the early, for Buchanan even in the late, sixteenth century. More habitually composed in Latin, even when he meant to be printed in English; Erasmus and Buchanan both composed and published in Latin exclusively. The literary achievement of the vernaculars had challenged the Latin primacy. But, thought the humanists, that rivalry had been possible only because the primacy had been misused. Latin primacy to them was an article of literary faith, a dogma. It must not lapse; and to restore its authority all they needed was to restore its classical diction. No, says modern linguistic science in retrospect, that was a delusion; it could only segregate Latin farther. In fact Latin declined, slowly and as if inevitably, from a primary language to a secondary. But those who now mock the humanists for blindly hastening the decline of Latin to a "dead" language should remember that throughout the Renaissance itself Latin was active in every country and with almost every man of letters. It was far from dead; but it was no longer primary.

Evidently the scholars of the fifteenth and sixteenth centuries saw in the Latin literature of their time the revival of classical standards after medieval decadence. Rejecting the medieval experience, they were bent on restoring Latin to its classical eminence by reviving its classical forms and style. They proposed a new Latin literature in Augustan phrase.

Keeping its established place as the language of education, Latin continued to be thought of as a norm of permanence. As late as 1586 Montaigne, remembering his boyhood, says (III. ii) : "To me Latin is, as it were, natural; I understand it better than French." Later (1586–1588) he adds (III. ix) : "I am writing my book for a few men and a few years. If there had been any idea of its lasting, I must have committed it to a language of more stability." In other words, the vernaculars of course would continue to shift; not Latin. For by Latin the humanists meant the Latin of Vergil, Caesar, Sallust, above all of Cicero, the Latin of the great period. Renaissance humanism was a cult not merely of antiquity in general, but specifically of Augustan Latin. It sought to revive not only the ancient forms, but especially the ancient diction. The literary preoccupation of the Renaissance was with style. For the highest literary eminence, said the humanists, writing must be in Latin, that is in the superior language, and in Augustan Latin, that is in the style of the superior period.

The humanists demanded conformity, then, to Augustan diction. Lorenzo Valla's *Elegantiae linguae latinae* (1476), reprinted again and again, first of a long line of phrase books, and characteristic in its very title, was a guide to conformity. Beyond conformity ranged imitation. Humanistic Latin is imitative in theory, and in practice so various as to furnish abundance of significant examples. These various degrees and kinds will appear in subsequent chapters. Meantime the obvious practical warrant for imitation is in exercises. Imitation in any art is a recognized means of study by practice; it is not an end. But Renaissance enthusiasm for revival often made elegant conformity a goal in itself. An oration might seem an achievement by being Ciceronian, a pastoral dialogue by being Vergilian. The subject, the idea, the message of a speech, a letter, a poem might have little claim; nevertheless publication might be warranted by the style. To exhibit the elegant diction and the harmonious sentence-forms of the great period might seem sufficient distinction. "Thus the whirligig of time brings in his revenges." Posterity, instead of continuing to read such humanistic imitations, has long forgotten them. Few literary products have been less permanent than those of the cult of permanence. A pervasive danger in this classicism was its encouragement to a literature of themes.

2. GREEK

Even before the humanistic return to classical Latin another vista of the ancient world had been opened by the revival of Greek. Generally in abeyance through most of the Middle Age, Greek had been recovered in the fourteenth century and was well established in the early fifteenth. It was studied by both Boccaccio and Petrarch. It had its professor at the Florence *studium* (1396) in Chrysolaras, who went to England in 1400. Guarino, his pupil at Constantinople, after bringing Greek to Florence and Venice, settled (1431) at Ferrara, and attracted among his many famous pupils the Englishmen Gray, Free, Gunthorpe, and Tiptoft.[1] Bessarion was at the Council of Constance (1414). The fall of Constantinople (1453), sending many Greek exiles to Italy, merely increased opportunities already widely available. Even before the establishment of printing there was increasing circulation of manuscripts. Aurispa (1372–1460), for instance, besides being scholar and professor, was an active dealer. Printing came in the nick of time to spread the new vogue. There was a Florence text of Homer in 1488, an Aldus in 1504. Aristotle, besides being translated anew, had a Greek text in 1495 (Venice), another in 1503 (Paris). Sophocles was printed by Aldus in 1502. Even the earliest sixteenth century commanded texts of a considerable variety of Greek authors.

The variety, indeed, is striking. Evidently the humanistic cult of an ideal period of Latin did not guide the selection of Greek. All was fish that came to the Renaissance Greek net. Late Greek was as welcome as the Greek of the great dramatists and orators; Alexandrian, as epic. With the vogue of Plato in the fifteenth century came that of the neo-Platonists; with the texts and translations of Aristotle, Hermes Trismegistus; with Homer, the

[1] Allen, *Age of Erasmus*, p. 121.

Anthology and Apollonius Rhodius. Isocrates vied once more with Demosthenes. Nor did Sophocles oust Seneca, or Thucydides prevail against Livy. The wide and continued influence of sophistic appears in the vogue of Athenaeus, Hermogenes, Aphthonius, and even Libanius. Discrimination, indeed, was sometimes beyond Renaissance scholarship. Henri Étienne, one of the best Greek scholars of the sixteenth century, published (1554) a collection of Byzantine imitations which he supposed to belong to the time of Anacreon. This was the Anacreon that inspired Ronsard and was translated by Belleau. Since textual criticism was hardly understood before the seventeenth century, hardly formulated before the eighteenth, Renaissance printed texts are generally inaccurate.[2] Nevertheless to have Greek authors, classical and decadent, at first hand, to read the message in its own style, even imperfectly, was a literary experience and had some excitement of exploration.

Thus was opened more widely a literature recommended alike by the praise and by the imitation of the Augustan Romans. Habits of language and style outside the Latin tradition, for the first time in centuries, were made generally available. How far they availed, how far Greek operated as language, especially on the widening vernacular literatures, can better be gathered from the progress of this history than measured here in advance. At first view the influence seems extensive. Renaissance scholars as a matter of course at least professed to know

[2] É. Egger, *L'Hellénisme en France* (Paris, 1869), pp. 358–359; see Monnier, II, 134 for modern estimate of Renaissance Greek texts.

Greek; and most authors at least professed to be scholars. Poliziano was both; and his knowledge of Greek seems to have been solid. In 1485 his *Oratio in expositione Homeri* thus compliments his university audience on its command of Greek.

You are those Florentines in whose city all Greek learning, long extinct in Greece itself, has so revived and flourished that both your men expound Greek literature in public lectures and the youths of your highest nobility, as never has happened in Italy for a thousand years, speak Attic so purely, so easily and smoothly, that Athens, instead of being sacked and seized by barbarians, seems itself, of its own will wrenched away with its own soil and, so to speak, with all its furniture, to have immigrated to Florence and there entirely and intimately to have founded itself anew (Gryphius edition, Lyon, 1537–1539, III. 63–64).

The obvious exaggeration of an introductory public lecture does not lead him to quote Homer in Greek. The abundant examples are given in his Latin translation. Moreover this encomium of Homer relies not on specific considerations of Greek language and style, but on such conventional topics as could be derived equally well from a translation. The writing of Greek, in spite of occasional published efforts, is probably measured with his usual justice by Bembo. "We study Greek not to use it, except for exercise, but the better to explore Latin."[3] Poliziano, in spite of his Greek and of his youthful achievement in Italian verse, wrote the bulk of his work in Latin prose. Rabelais from his monastery at Fontenay-le-Comte (1521) invoked the help of Budé toward procuring

[3] *Prose,* I, vi (1525).

Greek books; he translated a Greek author who had already been translated; but how much Greek he achieved is hard to determine. Of Julius Caesar Scaliger, whose Greek was one of his warrants for vanity, Egger says: "though he knows much Greek, he seems to know it ill."[4] The same critic records of Henri Étienne: "From the age of fifteen he knew and spoke Greek almost as his native language, and better than Latin."[5] Ronsard's imitation of Greek verse is based on knowledge of the Greek language. Montaigne, saturated in Plutarch, tells us that he knows no Greek. His Plutarch is the translation of Amyot; and from Amyot, not from the Greek text of Longus, is derived the vogue of *Daphnis and Chloe*. Both the extent and the character of Greek influence may more safely be estimated thus from individual literary forms and even from individual authors.

One general influence may be guessed from the stimulus given by Greek to the Renaissance vogue of mythology. Boccaccio had already, in his *Genealogia deorum gentilium*[6] ranged beyond Ovid; and in the sixteenth century such manuals as Natale Conti's (Natalis Comes) *Mythologiae* (1580) were in active demand. Mythology equipped the poetry not only of printed books, but also of pageants and solemn entries. It was so widely pervasive as to seem almost obligatory. But how much of this vogue was due to Greek? Greek mythology had been in ancient times largely taken over into Latin. The dis-

[4] Egger, p. 398.
[5] *Ibid.*, p. 205.
[6] Edition of Osgood, pp. 119, 193.

tinctively Greek habit, that is the earlier mythological habit, is to feel and treat the myth not merely as a conventional allusion, but as a perennial story. For the literary use of mythology is twofold. Either it is decorative, one of the ornaments of style, or it is itself a form of poetry. The latter, the perennial recreation of Prometheus or Medea, was less conspicuous in Latin poetry than in Greek. How far the revival of Greek brought it back may here and there be divined. It never quite dies. The widespread medieval story of Mélusine is essentially identical with Medea, though it did not come through Greek. On the other hand, Ariosto's Angelica bound to the rock directly suggests Andromeda, though the myth reappears also in the popular ballad of *Kemp Owen*. Such myth-making gives a clue to Boccaccio's *Ameto*. There is something of it in Poliziano's *Orfeo*. It is carefully imitated from Pindar by Ronsard. It somewhat vaguely animates Spenser. But it is not common in the Renaissance. For the Renaissance generally, regarding mythology in the more usual way as a mine of stylistic ornament, was merely more anxious to have it standardized, to be sure that gods and goddesses wore the correct classical costumes. Diana in the *Venatio* (1512) of Adrian, Cardinal Corneto, is such a figure; and her attendant nymphs are as much part of the decoration as the chased bowls. Indeed, the Middle Age, frankly adapting ancient cults to its own time, had been nearer to the Greek habit. Chaucer had made the temple in his *Troilus and Criseyde* a cathedral, and called the Palladion a relic. While Renaissance painting was handling mythology in this free way, Renaissance literature often used it merely as archaistic decoration.

Thus it appears in Francesco Colonna's fantastic allegory *Hypnerotomachia* (1467), and in its abundant woodcuts. The main figures, though they have Greek names, are allegorical in the fashion of the *Roman de la Rose*. The guide Logistica, for instance, is Reason; the other guide, Thelemia,[7] Desire or Will. The nymphs met at every turn serve for erotic suggestion; the Greek inscriptions, for decoration. Colonna's diction is studiously deformed by such Greek coinage as *lithoglypho, hypaethrio, chariceumati*. The precious style thus becomes a dilated pedantic jargon. In the whole preposterous book there is nothing Greek below the surface.

How far did Greek influence Renaissance thought? Aristotle had dominated the Middle Age in the Latin translations of Boethius and in Latin versions of the Arabs. The Renaissance retranslated him and published the Greek text. It restored him to challenge him. Were the Renaissance translations superior to those of Boethius, who was scholar and philosopher as well as poet? Did the Renaissance texts convey him more truly? Renaissance texts are often questionable; and Aristotle's *Poetic,* at least, was understood very slowly. The Renaissance welcomed Plato. Was it Plato? Why is Renaissance Platonism peculiarly difficult to measure, or even to define? Such questions are relevant here only to the revival of the Greek language. How far did this revival guide philos-

[7] Probably the source of Rabelais's Abbey of Thelème. He had read the book.

ophy? The question comes up incidentally in one of Sperone Speroni's earlier dialogues, *Dialogo delle lingue* (about 1540); and the answer is so unusual as to be startling. Philosophy has not been advanced by our study of Latin and Greek; it has been deviated. This sharp turn, in a dialogue discussing the superiority of Latin and Greek to the vernaculars, comes as a reminiscence of the teaching of Peretto.

Peretto (p. 121) used to say that the time spent on learning Latin and Greek actually hinders learning and developing philosophy. No language (p. 123) has in itself any peculiar value. Aristotle, therefore, not only may be studied in Latin, but might be studied in Italian. In fact (p. 126), language studies may be illusory, as we see around us. "I grieve at the wretched condition of these modern times, in which study is spent not in being, but in seeming wise. . . We think we know something well enough when, without comprehending its nature, we are able to give it the name given by Cicero, Pliny, Lucretius, Vergil, or Plato, Aristotle, Demosthenes, Aeschines." [8]

Hardly more than a parenthesis, this stands out as a challenge both of the superiority of Greek as a language and, more generally, of Renaissance confidence in language studies as a means of education.

Such challenges are rare. Bembo, in Speroni's dialogue, will not admit any such heresy as the equality of languages; nor, we may well assume, would Sperone himself admit that language study was hindering philosophy. For the Renaissance generally agreed that education should normally proceed through the study of languages. Of

[8] Page references to 1596 edition.

this the "new learning" was no less persuaded than the old. The newness consisted in revising the traditional Latin and in adding other languages, especially Greek. Louvain established (1518) the College of the Three Languages (Latin, Greek, and Hebrew); and the same name was at first commonly applied to the Collège de France (1530). Though this royal foundation was effectually new in other aspects that now may seem more important, its idea and inception came in great part from the movement for Greek in education. Nor did the movement stop with the individual college. Nothing more vividly exemplifies Renaissance preoccupation with language studies than the addition of Greek to the university curriculum. Thwarted, in a time of bitter controversy, by the association of Greek with Protestantism, the cause was won before the end of the century. The prescription promulgated officially in 1600, and the educational theory behind it, held substantially for three hundred years. There, at least, is a permanent result of the Renaissance.

3. THE VERNACULARS

(a) Italian

The humanist assertion of the literary superiority of Latin did not pass unchallenged even in the fifteenth century. Alberti (1404–1472), scholar and philosopher, insisted that actual communication, the conveying of a message, should be in the vernacular, and set an example by writing many of his learned works in Italian. Though humanists might disparage even so great a succession as Dante, Petrarch, and Boccaccio, and in the languid period some promising ambitions might be deviated into Latin, by the sixteenth century the literary rights of the vernacular were both recovered in practice and acknowledged in theory. The shift of opinion is significantly recorded by Bembo. Elegant Latinist, accomplished poet in the vernacular, judicious critic, he posed in an Italian literary dialogue (*Prose,* Venice, 1525), Giuliano de' Medici, Federigo Fregoso, and Hercole Strozza discussing the capacity of Italian style:

I. Our vernacular, most explored and perfected at Florence, is more intimate to us than Latin, as to the Romans Latin was than Greek (i-iv). Yes, but as Greek was then superior, so Latin is now. Answer (v): if that implied that the superior should always be cultivated, nobody would ever have written well in his own language. As Cicero sought to augment the authority of his own Latin, so did Dante, Petrarch, and Boccaccio for Italian. Greek (vi) we may dismiss, since it is not a medium for us; we study it not to use it, but the better to explore Latin. Provençal (vii-xi), though once an important language of literature and very influential in our early poetry, has been superseded by Italian.

But if we are to use the vernacular for literature, *which* vernacular? (xii) Italian is not uniform. Shall we adopt the language of the Papal Court? No; it has not writers enough to constitute literary authority. Tuscan (xiii-xv) is best, as having shown amplest capacity, and as actually holding the literary leadership.

Shall we incline, then, to its older usage, or to current popular speech? Answer (xvi-xvii): we are not limited to this dilemma. We may cultivate a diction that remains acceptable. Cicero or Demosthenes made himself entirely intelligible to the populace without speaking as the populace would have spoken to him.

II. An historical review (xx) of Italian poetry to and from Dante finds all its graces united in Petrarch. So (xxi) all previous prose writers were surpassed by Boccaccio. No subsequent writers have equalled these two. Meantime Latin has been so freed from the rust of ignorant centuries that today it has regained its ancient splendor and charm.

In an analysis (xxiii-xxviii) of style under the classical headings, Dante (xxiv) is rebuked for base words. He might better have left out the things.

The qualities of vowels and of consonants (xxvii-xxviii), and the three kinds of rhyme (xxix), with examples from Petrarch, lead to a discussion of rhythm (*numero,* xxxii-xxxiii), quantity (*tempo,* xxxv), and variation. The conclusion reaffirms the preëminence of Petrarch and Boccaccio.

III. The noble works of Michael Angelo and of Raphael should spur us to a like achievement in literature. This final section discusses Tuscan in detail: word-forms, inflection, syntax, and especially usage.

The dialogue opens a vista into contemporary thought about style. The objection to Dante's base words, startling to us now, was made frequently then. No less characteristic of the time is the homage to Petrarch as great poet and as master of style. Giraldi Cinthio expressed the common view in a flowery simile.

But the law is not so strict for romances as not to permit more license in words than is customary for sonnets and canzoni. Long and serious subjects, if the conception is not to be warped, need such latitude, which must nevertheless be limited. Petrarch shows this clearly in his *Trionfi.* I will not cite Dante; for whether through the fault of his age, or because of his own nature, he took so many liberties that his liberty became a fault. Therefore I find quite judicious that painter who, to show us in a fair scene the literary value of the one poet and the other, imagined both in a green and flowery mead on the slopes of Helicon, and put into Dante's hand a scythe, which, with his gown tucked up to his knees, he was wielding in circles, cutting every plant that the scythe struck. Behind Dante he painted Petrarch, in senatorial robe, stooping to select the noble plants and the well-bred flowers— all this to show us the liberty of the one and the judgment and observance of the other (*Discorsi,* Venice, 1554, pp. 133–134).

What Bembo calls Tuscan was at once a fact and an ideal. It is the current name not only for the diction of Tuscany, but for the literary diction increasingly practiced by all writers in Italian. Castiglione feels himself bound to defend certain Lombard words. Ariosto anxiously re-vises to conform. Tasso has a dispute with the *Accademia della Crusca.* The most distinct dialect was in Naples. To conform to Tuscan was for Neopolitans most nearly like acquiring another language. But even there, and much more readily in other parts of Italy, Tuscan was accepted and increasingly practiced as literary Italian. Used by scholars who also wrote Latin, Italian naturally learned from Cicero and Vergil more logical and rhythmical sentence habits, more adroit shaping of verse. Thus the best result of humanism, perhaps, was the one least sought by the humanists, the refinement of the vernacular.

Lodovico Dolce's *Observations on the Vernacular* (Venice, 1550) is an Italian grammar addressed to edu-cated readers and using the classical headings. A section (157–186) on punctuation shows both the new emphasis demanded by printing and a shift of control from rhythm toward logic. Nearly fifty pages are devoted to Italian verse forms. Though there are many examples from Boccaccio and a few from other authors, the great exemplar throughout is Petrarch. Petrarch, then, was a model for Italian poetry, Boccaccio for prose. As humanist Latin had its thesaurus, so the cult of native models should have wherewith to guide both study and imitation. Francesco Alunno's *Observations on Petrarch* (1539) is a concordance plus a text of the sonnets and canzoni. His concordance of Boccaccio's *Decameron* (1543) has the significant title *The Riches of the Vernacular*. Finally *The Frame of the World* (*Della fabrica del mondo*, 1546–1548) is entitled further "ten books containing the words of Dante, Petrarch, Bembo, and other good authors, by means of which writers may express with ease and eloquence all man's conceptions of any created thing whatsoever." The ten divisions are God, heaven, the world, the elements, the soul, the body, man, quality, quantity, and hell. On this grandiose scale the thesaurus carried out for mature writers in the vernacular the idea of contemporary schoolbooks for Latin themes. It was indeed a *copia*.

(b) French

Italian theory of the vernacular being typical generally, and being moreover quickly known in France, the progress of French thought need not be detailed. Jean Lemaire allegorized *La Concorde des deux langages* (about 1512) to urge Frenchmen and Italians together from lower to higher poetry. No less than Italy France saw its literary future in the vernacular. But France had not so compelling a literary past. Its fourteenth century had no such mighty succession as Dante, Petrarch, and Boccaccio. Its medieval greatness was more remote; its medieval survivals, generally languid. So the more ardent of coming French poets were ready to repudiate not only medieval Latin for classical Latin, but also medieval French verse for a new, classical French poetry. The promotion of this is the movement called the Pléiade; and its manifesto is Joachim du Bellay's *Deffense et illustration de la langue française* (1549).

The main idea is so to *enrich* French diction as to establish an equality with Greek and Latin. This is the meaning of *illustration* in the title. More than a century later Dryden used the same Latin root for the same idea when he said that medieval English poetry lacked *lustre*. Greek or Latin, Du Bellay urges, has no such linguistic superiority as to compel our using it as our own literary medium. Cultivation of the classics as languages leads to pedantry. Philosophy is not a language study. Those who so pursue it seem more anxious to show learning than to have it. For a literary career, indeed, one must know Latin and preferably Greek also, but not as an end and not as a medium of expression. Latin and Greek, then, have their value in the writer's education, not in his writing; but Du Bellay does not draw this inference explicitly, and seems not to see the further inference that the real enriching is not of one's language, but of oneself. For he proposes that French be improved by classical grafts, and further by imitation of classical style. Let us enhance

French literature, he urges, by making French language more classical.

Thus to reduce the treatise to its lowest terms is quite unjust to its suggestiveness. But its intrinsic value at best is less than its historical. Ignoring a French medieval achievement already forgotten or misunderstood, it turns humanist imitation toward giving French poetry classical lustre.

Such manipulation was unchecked by any considerable knowledge of the actual development of language. Even the learned Benedictine, Périon, derived French from Greek (*Ioachimi Perionii Benedictini. . . dialogorum de linguae gallicae origine, eiusque cum graeca cognatione, libri quatuor,* Paris, 1555; dedication dated 1554).

Périon is cautious in his conclusions, as in his title. He has unusual grasp of phonetic cognates: b, f, p, v (p. 54); t, d, th (p. 107 verso); c, ch, g, k (p. 125). He admits, of course, the large influence of Latin. But he seems to think that Gallic derived directly from Greek, and added its abundant Latin later. What he cites in his parallels is not Celtic, but French. Though the historical introduction is negligible, the linguistic proof, even where it is in error, shows both awareness of language processes and some scientific knowledge.

French is like Greek, he finds, in the habit of articles (p. 107), in accent (p. 111), in nouns ending -on and te, in having an aorist (p. 134), in using the infinitive as a verbal noun (p. 135). Thus though his theory and many of his particular derivations are unsound, his method of observing language habits is ahead of his time. Citing Budé, Baif, and a few Latin authors, he seems in the main to have worked independently from his own observations.

That so much knowledge of detail should reach so little grasp of the whole shows the prevailing ignorance of linguistic science.

The last quarter of the sixteenth century raised among the vernaculars the question of rank. Enthusiasm for the theory and the achievement of Italian had led some Frenchmen, in spite of the triumphs of Ronsard, to disparage their own. In 1579, thirty years after Du Bellay's manifesto, Henri Étienne (Henricus Stephanus), scholar and editor, sought not only to vindicate French rights, but to demonstrate French superiority, in his book on the *Preëminence of the French Language* (*Project du livre entitulé De la précellence du langage françois*).[9]

Under the headings weight (*gravité*, p. 196), charm (*grace*, p. 217), and range (*richesse*, p. 246) he proposes to prove (p. 176) that "our French language surpasses all the other vernaculars." Spanish he dismisses (p. 179) as evidently inferior to Italian, and hence to French. English is not even mentioned. The demonstration is of French superiority to Italian.

First (p. 181), French is more stable. We have never needed "grands personnages" to tell Frenchmen how to use French. Where they have occasionally done so for pleasure, they have not left us in the dark with their disputes. The objection that we are not agreed as to which

[9] Edited by Louis Humbert, Paris, 1914.

part of France has standard French, nor as to how it should be spelled, is rebutted. French and Italian translations of the same original (p. 204) are put side by side. It is noteworthy that Ronsard (pp. 207–208) in each case dilates.

In detail, Italian inflectional endings lead to monotony (p. 218); and Italian word-forms are not consistently adapted from the Latin. French is richer in diminutives (p. 241), in its legacy (p. 260) from medieval romances and crafts, and (p. 314) in proverbs. Its facility in adaptation (p. 280) appears especially in compounds.

An Italian of equal learning could readily counter on each of these points. Could he disprove the whole? Could he prove the superiority of Italian? Can any language be proved superior to all others? As between two modern languages, the preference, many would say, is grounded not on demonstration, but on taste and habit. Italian cannot be proved superior or inferior to Spanish, French to English. Each writer naturally prizes the language that he knows best above another that he knows less. Étienne's thesis is not susceptible of proof. Perhaps; but what of Greek and Latin? Some men even today, far more in the Renaissance, would offer to prove that Greek is a superior language. For Étienne's treatise raises in a new quarter an old question that even now is not answered unanimously.

Whatever one's attitude toward this larger question, and however unconvincing Étienne may seem, his treatise is not absurd; nor is it a Renaissance *tour de force*. It is both serious and learned. Latinist and Hellenist, exact in the fine tradition of his house, he had the right to speak on language. His citing (p. 288) of historical consonant change shows some inkling, most uncommon in his time, of linguistic science. But in 1579 he could not know linguistic sufficiently. He assumes, as Du Bellay does, that processes of language are largely conscious, even deliberate choice (pp. 224, 400). His assumption that Provençal is French (Bembo had assumed that it was Italian) is not mere begging of the question. No one of his time could know the historical processes by which Provençal, Tuscan, Spanish, northern French, not to mention other tongues, had evolved from Latin. Even so, some of his citations of forms still have linguistic value. The larger value is in the literary discrimination of his wide reading, in the ingenious device of parallel translations, and in the significance of a dispute that was bound to recur as each vernacular came to represent more and more a national self-consciousness.

(c) English

National self-consciousness became notorious in England with the Elizabethans. Even with them lingers a certain nervousness as to the capacity of the English language. Such doubts arose not only from humanistic exaltation of Latin, but even more from ignorance of linguistic history. The barren fifteenth century had at least established the language of London as the English literary norm. The northern speech indiscriminately called Scotch, though its literary use persisted through the sixteenth century, came to be regarded as a dialect. The language of Malory's *Morte d'Arthur,* and generally of Caxton's publications, is substantially the same as that of the *Canterbury Tales*. By the time of Surrey, England had its Tuscan. Sixteenth-century literary usage in England, though its emergence from the barren period may seem slower than in Italy and France, is hardly more lax. The recklessness of Skelton, as the later recklessness of Rabelais, was individual extravagance. The vagaries of Spenser are not reckless; they are deliberate archaism. Where they violate the language of Chaucer, they show merely that a Renaissance poet who knew Latin and Greek, as well as French and Italian, might remain unaware of linguistic history, even in his own language. If the printed texts that he used had been more accurate, he might still have been too bent on following the lead of the Pléiade in manipulating language toward a new poetry to notice the difference between an infinitive and a preterit. For him Chaucer's words were color and sound, not forms. But though he misread Middle English, he felt too deeply what Ascham missed altogether, the tradition of English poetry, to dally long with classicizing metric. There had been no one to do for Chaucer what Alunno had done for Petrarch. Nevertheless, even without the help of good lexicons and grammars, Renaissance English shows a sufficient continuity of literary acceptance.

Prose, of course, lingered behind verse. Chaucer's prose rendering of Boethius, in sharpest contrast to his verse, had been groping. Malory's prose was sufficient for narrative, though not for such philosophical discussion. Prose control in both narrative and discussion seems assured first in Sir Thomas More; but as late as John Lyly the progress of prose was still uncertain. The brief vogue of "Euphuism" shows an attempt to "enrich" the vernacular by Latin sentence figures. Lyly came to recognize that the vernacular had its own literary ways and its own literary rights. Finally from being a court writer he turned to whole-hearted pursuit of the actual vernacular in order to win the larger audience. For the idea of changing one's native language by classical grafts or other literary manipulation, though it was unchecked by any accurate or extensive linguistic science,[10] gradually gave way before the facts of literary experience.

[10] Sir John Cheke, however, spoke as a scholar when he wrote to Hoby: "I am of opinion that our own tung shold be written cleane and pure, vnmixt and vnmangeled with borrowing of other tunges." Quoted in Arber's Introduction to Ascham's *Scholemaster*, p. 5.

Chapter III

IMITATION OF PROSE FORMS, CICERONIANISM, RHETORICS

I. ORATIONS, LETTERS, DIALOGUES

RENAISSANCE classicism is most obvious in adoption of prose forms. Orations, letters, dialogues, first in Latin, then in the vernaculars, studiously conform. Orations were none the less a preoccupation because they had little to do with affairs. Actual Renaissance conduct of government soon left little room for moving the people to action by oratory. Legal pleading, as always, had its special technic. But the oratory of occasion, that third type which marks anniversaries, extols achievements, and commemorates great men, was invited widely and cultivated classically. It embraces most of the published oratory of the Renaissance, and was practiced by most of the humanists in Latin. Leonardo Bruni of Arezzo (Leonardo Aretino) is typical both as official orator of Florence and in his early imaginary orations. Agostino Dati of Siena delivered an encomium of Eusebius (*De laudibus D. Eusebii presbyt. Stridonensis et Ecclesiae maximi doctoris, in ejus solemniis publice habita, anno 1446*). The funeral of Cardinal Bessarion at Rome had a Latin oration by the Cardinal Capranica. Jacopo Caviceo cast his congratulatory address to Maximilian on the victory (1490) over King Ladislaus of Bohemia in the form called *prosopopoeia,* that is, of imaginary addresses by Babylon, Troy, Byzantium, Carthage, and Rome (*Urbium dicta ad Maximilianum Federici Tertii Caesaris filium Romanorum regem triumphantissimum,* Parma, 1491). The Cologne collection, *Orationes clarorum virorum,*[1] made such oratory available for study and imitation.

Of the Italian orations collected by Francesco Sansovino (Venice, 1561, including some translations) as representative of his time, only one fifth are political, and these only to the extent of being hortatory. The rest are all occasional: nine funeral orations, a Christmas address, two before an academy, a call to high aim, a praise of Italian, four congratulations, and four imaginary addresses (*prosopopoeiae*). Claudio Tolomei has two imaginary orations, one for, the other against.[2] Such oratory, of course is perennial. Its Renaissance vogue is distinctive only in being almost exclusive and in being imitative. Bartolomeo Ricci records[3] that on two occasions in his office of public orator at Ferrara he imitated specific orations of Cicero. The habit was general. The desire to sound classical led even to the lifting of Augustan phrases and cadences. Similar conditions had led the decadent Greek oratory called sophistic[4] into archaism as a means of display. Renaissance oratory, even when it was not

[1] Parodied by *Orationes obscurorum virorum* (before 1515), which was part of the Reuchlin-Pfefferkorn controversy.

[2] This is the exercise called by the ancients *declamatio.* See ARP (*Ancient Rhetoric and Poetic*) and a letter of Erasmus, May 1, 1506.

[3] *Bartholomaei Riccii De imitatione libri tres* (Venice, 1545), folio 38 verso. See below, Chapter III, Sect. 3.

[4] MRP (*Medieval Rhetoric and Poetic*) I and II.

led further into the sophistic sacrifice of the message to the speaker, was thus habitually literary. In Latin especially it was less often a means of persuasion than an imitative literary form.

What the Latin oration might nevertheless attain was exhibited by the lectures of Poliziano and again in the range of Marc Antoine Muret (Muretus, 1525–1585). From a conventional *praelectio* on the *Aeneid* (1579) Muret turned to Tacitus (1580), not only with lively vigor, but with penetrative suggestion and urgent sentences. When he returned to official oratory for the feasts of St John Evangelist (1582) and the Circumcision (1584), he kept the suggestiveness within the obligatory pattern. True to their kind, models of conciseness, these have also their own appeal. Occasional oratory in the Renaissance, then, might be a literary achievement and a literary progress. More generally it was but one evidence of the Renaissance preoccupation with rhetoric.

No less inevitable among the published works of the humanists are their collected Latin letters. Since these had been carefully composed and revised, they might serve not only history, but literature. Sometimes in effect essays, sometimes almost orations, they are sometimes themes. The favorite model is Cicero; and in extreme cases the letter seems to consist of style. It is hardly a letter; it is an exercise. But thus to label Renaissance letter-writing generally would be grossly unfair. Poliziano's letter to Paolo Cortesi is admirable as a letter, and comes into literary history on that ground. For so letters have entered literature in any time. A Latin letter of

John of Salisbury[5] lifts the heart and fills the eyes. Its cadences are studiously conformed to the *cursus* of the Curial *dictamen;* its diction is expertly chosen to strike always by appeal and suggestion, never by violence; its hazardous course steers between Scylla and Charybdis because it is constantly shaped to its goal. For all this skill is spent singly on making the truth prevail. A less important, but more famous English letter, Dr Johnson's to the Earl of Chesterfield, is no less studious of style, no less expertly adjusted, even to the phrasing of the obligatory subscription, and no less single in its aim. Those who make light of such delicacy as mere style have much to learn both of letters and of literature. Among the works of Erasmus none is more important than his collected letters. The Renaissance did well to study Latin letters, and learned much. But it was mistaken in thinking that a letter reaches posterity except by reaching its original address and aim. The Latin letters of the Renaissance often betray a tendency to regard classical style as an end in itself. Such letters, written to be literary, give the impression that the Latin letter is a Renaissance literary form.

Perhaps the most popular of ancient prose forms in the Renaissance was the dialogue; for it was used even oftener in the vernaculars than in Latin, and became a favorite form of exposition. The Middle Age, of course, had many dialogues, but not of this sort. *Débat, estrif,*

[5] Ep. 221 in Migne's *Patrologia latina* (Vol. 199, p. 247), which dates it 1167; Ep. 223, p. 389, in the collection of the letters of Gerbert, John of Salisbury, and Stephen of Tournay printed by Ruette (Paris, 1611). The letter is translated MRP 209.

conflictus, amoebean eclogue were often allegorical and generally forms of poetry. Renaissance dialogue is typically prose discussion. Its vogue was evidently stimulated by the increasing availability of Plato in both translation and Greek text; but its method is not often his. The Platonic dialogue typically conveys the illusion of creative conversation. As Sperone Speroni observes,[6] it is a sort of prose that takes after poetry. It invites the reader to join a quest for truth, to feel his way with the speakers, to measure this objection, respond to that hint; and often it leaves him still guessing with them, still questing. The other ancient literary type of dialogue is Cicero's *De oratore.* This is less conversation than debate with definite argument, rebuttal, and progress to a conclusion.[7] Cicero's dialogue is not a quest; it is an exposition of something already determined, and it unfolds that by logical stages. Renaissance dialogue, having generally his object, turns oftener to his type; but it does not forget Plato. The more dramatic grouping of friends in converse appealed widely to Renaissance imagination. It was imitated in Platonic academies as well as in writing; and its form of dialogue opened more opportunities for exhibiting one's literary acquaintance and bringing forward one's literary friends. Further Renaissance dialogues did not often go with Plato. They stopped with the Platonic setting, or used challenges merely for transition. Even the most popular of them all, Castiglione's *Cortegiano,* though its *personae* are

---

[6] *Apologia dei dialoghi,* opening; p. 516 of the Venice, 1596, edition.

[7] For *De oratore,* see ARP.

unusually distinct, and though it concludes upon Platonic love, is evidently framed upon the *De oratore*. Platonic dialogue must be easy to read; it is by no means easy to write; witness the failure of many imitations, both Renaissance and modern. It is a very delicate adjustment of poetic to rhetoric. The grafting of Plato on Cicero demands long preparation. The usual Renaissance compromise of letting Plato introduce the speakers and Cicero rule their discourse was practically sufficient for the better Renaissance dialogues. The inferior ones have nothing but the externals of either. Their rejoinders, neither conversation nor debate, become tedious ceremony;[8] and their composition lacks the Ciceronian sequence. But even these show how widely the dialogue form was imitated from antiquity.

2. CICERONIANISM

The pervasive humanistic imitation was not adoption of forms; it was borrowing of style. The logical extreme of the humanist cult of Augustan Latin is the exclusive imitation of Cicero as the ideal of prose style. In 1422 Gherardo Landriani, Bishop of Lodi, drew from a long-forgotten chest in the cathedral library a complete manuscript of the principal works of Cicero on rhetoric. The *De oratore* and the *Orator* are the most mature and suggestive treatment of oratory by the greatest Roman orator. "*Summe gaudeo,* I have the greatest delight," wrote Poggio on receiving the news in London; and Niccolo

---

[8] Minturno, *Arte poetica,* is mere catechism. Perionius hardly achieves dialogue at all; his interlocutors merely interrupt.

de'Niccoli of Florence promised a copy to Aurispa in Constantinople. So widely was the world of scholarship stirred. For the recovery of the greater Cicero directly stimulated Renaissance classicism. In the Middle Age Cicero had been rather a name of honor than a literary influence. His *De inventione,* a common source of medieval rhetoric, is only a youthful compend. What was usually added for further study, especially of style, the *Rhetorica ad Herennium,* was ascribed to him quite erroneously. His greater works on rhetoric were appreciated doubtless here and there, as by John of Salisbury, but not generally. Hence the recovery of the *De oratore* in 1422 was indeed an event in the history of literature. This and *Orator* are fine encomia of the higher function of oratory, and of the orator as leader. Neither is a manual. Both in Cicero's intention are contributions to the philosophy of rhetoric. Without very original or even very specific doctrine they are eloquently persuasive. What did the Renaissance do with them?

Most obviously it carried classicism to the extreme of Ciceronianism, that exclusive imitation which made Cicero the ideal of Latin prose, the perfect model. The doctrine involves certain characteristic assumptions: (1) that Latin, or any other language, attains in a certain historical period its ideal achievement and capacity, (2) that within such a great period style is constant, (3) that a language can be recalled from later usage to earlier in scholastic exercises, (4) that such exercises can suffice for personal expression, (5) that a single author can suffice as a model, even for exercises.

Medieval Latin had departed from classical usage because it was a living language, so widely active in communication as to grow. Men used it without being disconcerted by changes from place to place, from time to time. Such changes are inevitable so long as a language is used generally. Denotations are extended or contracted, connotations are modified or superseded, even by written use. Oral use adds changes in cadence. From the seventh century on through the Middle Age Latin was accentual. The speech tune of Cicero had faded; and no one had tried to resuscitate what had been supplanted by other cadences. The Latin hymns had carried medieval measures to the heights of poetry. Not till the seventeenth century did humanism succeed in having them revised classically; and fifty volumes have since been spent in recovering their medieval forms.[9] The extreme form of Renaissance classicism, by ignoring the historical development of language, tended to inhibit the use of Latin in immediate appeal.

So rigid a doctrine did not, of course, enlist all Renaissance humanists. The more judicious were content to select certain expert habits, especially Cicero's strong and supple wielding of sentences. But the extremists, such as Christophe de Longueil (Longolius, 1488–1522), got fame; the doctrine continued in teaching and in practice; and as late as 1583 there was point in Sidney's scornful allusion to "Nizolian paper books." His readers knew that he meant the use of the Cicero thesaurus as a handbook for composition. Even where it did not enlist

[9] *Analecta hymnica.*

devotees, Ciceronianism confirmed the prevalent idea of the standard diction of the great period. Yet before the end of the fifteenth century both the general assumption and the particular cult had been exploded by Poliziano. As university teacher, in the introductory lecture (*praelectio*) of his course at Florence on Quintilian and Statius, he challenged the doctrine of the ideal classical period by a plea for the pedagogical value of later Latin.

Finally I would not attach undue importance to the objection that the eloquence of these writers was already corrupted by their period; for if we regard it aright, we shall perceive that it was not so much corrupted and debased as changed in kind. Nor should we call it inferior just because it is different. Certainly it shows greater cultivation of charm: more frequent pleasantry, many epigrams, many figures, no dull realizations, no inert structure; all not so much sound as also strong, gay, prompt, full of blood and color. Therefore, though we may indisputably concede most to those authors who are greatest, so we may justly contend that some qualities which are earlier attained and much more attainable [i.e., by students] are found in these [minor authors]. So, since it is a capital vice to wish to imitate one author and him alone, we are not off the track if we study these before those, if we do some things for their practical use . . . [So, he adds, did Cicero himself when he turned from the Attic orators to the Rhodian and even to the Asiatic.] So that noble painter who was asked with what master he had made the most progress replied strikingly "With that one," pointing to the populace; yes, and rightly too. For since nothing in human nature is happy in every aspect, many men's excellences must be viewed, that one thing may stick from one, another thing from another, and that each [student] may adapt what suits him (*Opera,* Gryphius edition, Lyon, 1537–1539, III, 108–109).

Perhaps nothing else so pointed and telling against Ciceronianism was written during the Renaissance as Poliziano's letter to Paolo Cortesi.

Nor are those who are thought to have held the first rank of eloquence like one another, as has been remarked by Seneca. Quintilian laughs at those who shall think themselves cousins of Cicero because they conclude a period with *esse videatur.* Horace declaims against imitators who are nothing but imitators. Certainly they who compose only by imitation seem to me like parrots or magpies uttering what they do not understand. For what they write lacks force and life, lacks impulse, lacks emotion, lacks individuality, lies down, sleeps, snores. Nothing true there, nothing solid, nothing effective. But are you not, some one asks, expressing Cicero? What of it? I am not Cicero. I am expressing, I think, myself. Besides, there are some, my dear Paul, who beg their style, as it were bread, piecemeal, who live not only from the day, but unto the day. Thus unless they have at hand the one book to cull from, they cannot join three words without spoiling them by rude connection or disgraceful barbarism. Their speech is always tremulous, vacillating, ailing, in a word so ill cared and ill fed that I cannot bear them, especially when they pass judgment on those whose styles deep study, manifold reading, and long practice have as it were fermented. But to come back to you, Paul, of whom I am very fond, to whom I owe much, whose talent I value very highly, I am asking whether you so bind yourself by this superstition that nothing pleases you which is simply yours, and that you never take your eyes from Cicero. When you have read Cicero—and other good authors —much and long, worn them down, learned them by heart, concocted, filled your breast with the knowledge of many things, and are now about to compose something yourself, then at last I would have you swim, as the saying is, without corks, take sometimes your own advice, doff that too morose and anxious solicitude to make yourself merely a Cicero—in a word risk your whole strength (*Opera*, Gryphius edition, Lyon, 1537–1539, I, 251).

The writer of that letter, in spite of his youthful triumphs in the vernacular, gave his mature years to the writing of Latin and the teaching of Latin and Greek literature. Unfortunately his expert Latin did not move Renaissance classicism to abandon either the practice of Ciceronianism or the theory of the ideal great period.

Some forty years after the destructive analysis of Poliziano, Ciceronianism was still active enough to draw the satire of Erasmus in the *Dialogus Ciceronianus* (1528). This *reductio ad absurdum,* beginning with the error of using a Cicero thesaurus as a handbook for composing, proceeds to the affectation of using for the Christian religion the terms proper to classical paganism: Jupiter Optimus Maximus for God the Father, Apollo for the Christ. Erasmus amuses himself by thus rewriting the Apostles' Creed in Ciceronian terms. His point is not merely the pedantry of such paganism, nor its irreverence, but its unreality. Only the words can be taken over; the meaning or the suggestion, in one direction or the other, is violated. The point had been made more forcibly, because more practically, by Poliziano. Preoccupation with past usage thwarts the expression of actual present things and thoughts. Further Erasmus makes his Ciceronian admit that the cult is illusory, a dream which according to its own adepts has never quite come true. Incidentally the names thus brought up in the dialogue are not only of those Ciceronians who had at least a transient fame, but also of some whom history does not even know.

In spite of this destructive satire, Giulio Camillo reaffirmed Ciceronianism with undisturbed simplicity.

Latin is no longer spoken, as our vernacular is, or French; it has been shut up in books. Since we are limited to gathering it not from actual speech, but from books, why not rather from the perfect than from the inferior? Let us first recall the language to the state in which we may believe it to have been while Vergil wrote it, or Cicero, and then confidently use that, even as Vergil did, or Cicero? (*Trattato della imitatione*, 1544.)

In 1545 Bartolomeo Ricci, tutor to Hercole d'Este's son Lorenzo, closed his treatise *De imitatione* with a Ciceronian credo and a long defense of Longolius. Ciceronianism, then, survived both rebuttal and satire. As late as 1580 Muret, having renounced his own early Ciceronianism, attacked its major premise, the doctrine of the ideal great period. His argument is not, as Poliziano's a hundred years before, pedagogical; it is a direct challenge to Renaissance competence in judging Latin style. His previous *praelectio* had urged the distinctive claims of Tacitus: practical philosophy, finished economy of style. This second lecture on Tacitus deals with objections. The preference for Suetonius he merely dismisses. But Tacitus is accused of inaccuracy. By whom? By Vopiscus; and who is Vopiscus? Tacitus is hostile to the Christian religion. Shall we rule out all the pagans? The rest of the lecture deals with style.

There remain two objections brought against Tacitus by the inexpert: that his style is obscure and rough, and that he does not write good Latin. When I hear complaints of the obscurity of Tacitus, I reflect how easily people transfer their own faults to others. [I remember the anecdote of the man who complained that the windows were too small, when the real trouble was his own failing sight. So a deaf man was heard to complain that people did not speak distinctly.]

But Tacitus, says another, is rough. Alciati, praising his friend Jovius, has not feared to call the histories of Tacitus thorny. Well, praising Jovius shows as much judgment as blaming Tacitus. No two could be more different. Tacitus could not but displease a man who made so much of Jovius. . . For Jovius is all smooth; he has not a trace of that roughness which offends Alciati in Tacitus. He not only flows; he overflows. . . As Alciati is afraid of roughness, I am sick of silliness. Sirup for babes; but let me have a bowl of something with a tang.

Finally, those who grant to Tacitus his other qualities still deplore his bad Latin. The first movers of this calumny, each of whom had spent much pains in expounding Tacitus, were Alciati and Ferret. If they themselves wrote Latin as well as they think, perhaps we might be disturbed by their authority. Do you make bold, some one may say, to judge such men? They have made bold to judge Tacitus. . . [If we can know Latin (as Camillo says) only from books (and, we may add, from comparatively few books), we have the less warrant for judging Latin usage.] . . . Who dare affirm for certain today, when "the old authors" are so extolled, that the questioned phrases of Tacitus were never used by these "old authors?" (Leipzig ed. of 1660, vol. II, pp. 108–112.)

Even now, perhaps, though the name of the heresy has long been forgotten, the Ciceronian perversion of imitation is not extinct. But if this kind of imitation is not valid, what kinds are valid? Imitation of style may be suggestive when it remains subconscious, not the recalling of words, but the adaptation of remembered rhythms. The deliberate conformity proposed by Ciceronianism can be useful only as exercise, as the learning of certain effects by trying them. Once learned, these become an added resource in revision. In composing, in the creative process of bringing one's message to one's audience, deliberate imitation of style has no warrant. It would at least interrupt, and might deviate or inhibit. In so far as Ciceronianism confuses two processes normally separate, composing and revising, it tends to make style stilted.

Further, Ciceronianism narrows imitation by a theory of perfectionism. The *Imitatio Christi* (about 1460) is the direct appeal of an author preoccupied with his message. Sébastien Châteillon (1515–1563) rewrote its spontaneous Latin in Ciceronian cadences. It was imperfect; he would make it perfect. If this was pedantic, even absurd, wherein? If the *Pilgrim's Progress* should not be rewritten in the style of Hooker or of Sir Thomas Browne, why? Because *the* one ideal style is an illusion.

Finally, imitation need not be of style; it may be of composition; and for writing addressed to an actual public this is at once more available and more promising. For real writing, that is for a message intended to move the public, imitation generally risks less, and gains more, in guiding the plan, the whole scheme, the sequence. Renaissance preoccupation with style and tolerance of published themes tended to obscure the larger opportunity.

But there is no Ciceronianism in Castiglione's adopting the form of Cicero's *De oratore* for his *Cortegiano*. Though he naturally shows awareness of Cicero's expert periods, he is bent not on conformity of style, but on focusing the typical man of his own time in the literary frame used by Cicero for the typical Augustan Roman. Renaissance imitation of Vergil's style was often futile; but Tasso's *Jerusalem* was animated and guided by Vergil's epic sequence. Robert Garnier, imitating the style of Euripides, missed the dramatic composition; but Corneille caught the whole scheme of a Greek tragedy. Such larger imitation imposes no restraint on originality. Its recognition of ancient achievement is in practical adaptation to one's own conception and object and time. In this direction the classicism of the seventeenth century became more fruitful than that of the sixteenth.

3. RHETORICS

Manuals and treatises on rhetoric published in the fifteenth and sixteenth centuries exhibit marked differences in tradition, scope, and tendency. They range from narrow concentration on style to a full treatment of the five parts of rhetoric. They exhibit sophistic as well as rhetoric. Some persist in medieval preconception as others recover the classical heritage of Aristotle and Quintilian. The works mentioned below are typical of the many Renaissance manuals.

The *Rhetorica* (1437?) of George of Trebizond shows in brief the whole classical scope:[10] *inventio,* the explora-

[10] For the pattern of the classical rhetoric, see ARP.

tion of the subject and the determination of its *status;* *dispositio,* plan and order; *elocutio,* style; *memoria,* the art of holding a point for effective placing; and *pronuntiatio,* delivery. He is most expansive on the first, which had been both neglected and misapplied by the Middle Age.[11]

The presentation of rhetoric by Juan Luis Vives (*De ratione dicendi,* Bruges, 1532; reprinted in Vol. II of the Majansius edition of his works) is both meager and vaguely general.

Vives urges that rhetoric is not a study for boys, and that it should not be confined to diction. But he himself offers hardly anything specific about composition. Book I deals mainly with sentences (*compositio*), e.g., with dilation and conciseness as in the *Copia* of Erasmus, and with the period. Book II offers brief generalizations on type or tone of style, on the conventionalized measure of native ability against study and revision, on consideration of emotions and moral habits, on the threefold task of instructing, winning, and moving, and on appropriateness. Book III deals with narration (history, exempla, fables, poetry), paraphrase, epitome, commentary. History as composition is hardly even considered.

His incidental discussion of rheoric in *De causis corruptarum artium* and *De tradendis disciplinis* (Vol. VI of the collective edition) is no more satisfying. In Book IV of the former Vives so far misconceives the classical *inventio* as to rule it out of rhetoric altogether. Thus he practically ratifies the procedure of those Renaissance logicians who classified *inventio* and *dispositio* under logic. The classification was not a reform; it merely

[11] MRP.

recorded tardily the medieval practice of reducing rhetoric to style by relying for all the active work of composition on debate. Yet Vives pays repeated homage to both Aristotle and Quintilian.

On the other hand the concise manual of Joannes Caesarius (*Rhetorica,* Paris, 1542) returns to the full classical scope. The source cited most explicitly and quoted most frequently is Quintilian.

But that later ancient tradition called sophistic, which had deviated the rhetoric of the Middle Age, had also its Renaissance revival. Giulio Camillo (1479–1550), known in France as well as in Italy, published together a treatise on the orator's material, the oratorical fund, and another on imitation (*Due trattati . . . l'uno delle materie che possono venir sotto lo stile dell'eloquente, l'altro della imitatione,* Venice, 1544–1545). His constant preoccupation is with the topics, headings, commonplaces (*loci*) which guide the writer's preparation. Such are the headings of the sophistic recipe for encomium: birth and family, native city, deeds, etc. But sophistic had elaborated such obvious suggestions for exploring one's material into a system applicable both to material and to style. Camillo's source is:

the *Ideas* of Hermogenes, who in each considers eight things: the sense, the method, the words, the verbal figures, the clauses, their combination, sentence-control (*fermezza*), and rhythm. But my method is perhaps easier, since I proceed not from the forms (*forme*) to the materials, but from the materials to the forms . . . I have sought how many things can combine to produce the forms, and I find (as I have argued in my Latin orations) not eight things, as Hermogenes writes, but fourteen which may enter to modify any material. They are these: conceptions, or inventions (*Trovati*), passions, commonplaces, ways of speaking (*le vie del dire*), arguments, order, words, verbal figures, clauses, connectives, sentence forms, cadence (*gli estremi*), rhythms, harmonies.

This bewildering cross-division might serve as the *reductio ad absurdum* of the system of bringing on eloquence by topics if Camillo had not gone even further in a grandiose symbolistic scheme entitled *L'idea del theatro* (Florence, 1550). The theater here is not any actual stage; it is the manifold pageant of the world presented allegorically by topics for all literary purposes.

Starting from the medieval, or perhaps the neo-Platonic, premise that sacred things are not revealed, but figured, he divides his book into seven *gradi*. Seven is the perfect number; e.g., seven planets, Isaiah's seven columns, Vergil's *terque quaterque*, etc. Each *grado* is named after a planet, whose attributes are a mixture of astrology and mythology, as in the Middle Age, but again with a suggestion of orientalized Platonism. This general scheme constitutes the first section. The second is entitled *Il convivio;* the third, *l'Antro;* etc. A figure may appear in more than one *grado.*

Referring to this book in his treatise on imitation, he says: "By topics and images I have arranged all the headings that may suffice to group and to subserve all human conceptions." In the same treatise he even thinks of painting and sculpture as proceeding by topics: genus, sex, age, function, anatomy, light and shadow, attitude and action, adaptation to place. Topics can no farther go. Camillo's system, moreover, hardly touches composition;

all its manifold application is to style. Thus the more readily he accepts the common Renaissance confusion of poetic with rhetoric.

Another Ciceronian treatise on imitation is Bartolomeo Ricci's (*Bartholomaei Riccii de imitatione libri tres ad Alfonsum Atestium Principem, suum in literis alumnum, Herculis II Ferrariensium Principis filium* . . . Venice, 1545). Written ostensibly for the guidance of his pupil Alfonso, it is a discussion, not a textbook; but in the back of the author's mind is the prevalent conception of writing Latin as writing themes. The examples quote prose and poetry side by side without distinction of poetic from rhetoric. The usual complimentary references to contemporaries and to recognized previous humanists give the schoolmaster opportunity to exhibit his wide acquaintance. Poliziano is cited as challenging imitation; but his arguments are not given, nor the fact that his challenge was of Ciceronianism. Instead of citing his letter to Cortesi, Ricci merely praises Cortesi's reply as elegant. The *Ciceronianus* of Erasmus is similarly dismissed as an attack on Longueil. The progress of the book is generally from definition of imitation (I) through application of it in composition (II) to application in style (III). Ciceronianism, implied throughout, first in classicism, then by increasing use of Cicero as a model, is explicitly declared in III and supported by a long defense of Longueil.

I. Imitation, practiced in all human activities, is accepted in literature. Though Catullus in the marriage of Thetis and in the desolation of Ariadne said the last word and every word, nevertheless Vergil imitated him in Dido; and each has his own merits. [The Catullus passages are stock citations of the period.] Cicero and Vergil both counseled and practiced imitation. Why reduce following nature to following yourself? Following nature demands no more than being natural, i.e., verisimilitude. [The quibble here between nature in the sense of human nature and nature in the sense of one's own nature (*ingenium*) is unpardonable. Further, it is not clear what either has to do with imitation.] Imitate the best authors, each in his own kind. There follows a summary of Latin literature. [The book supplies no distinct definition of imitation as a means of advancing literary control. It shows, quite superfluously, that imitation is prevalent in the arts; it does not define the limits and the methods of practicing it in writing.]

II. A review of the revival of Augustan diction in a long list of humanists proves nothing specific concerning imitation, much concerning pride in humanistic Latin. Scholars, however, are not well paid. Doctors and lawyers write bad Latin. Teachers are incompetent. The vernacular has come even into the schools; and even Cicero is translated. Let us all combine to save Latin style. Imitation is not repetition, not copy; there must be variation. Imitation with Plautus and Terence was the taking of Greek plots [a very inexact account]. Vergil imitated Homer even to the lifting of passages, and made a better tempest. Cicero imitated the Greek orators. Vergil used the *Pharmaceutria* of Theocritus. [He did not imitate it.] Vergil's use of Cato and Varro adds beauty of style. [Is this imitation, or simply use of material?] Sallust's Catiline is admirable; but it did not preclude Cicero's. So, even after Lucretius, Ovid and Vergil treated the gods. [Here is mere confusion. Cicero did not imitate Sallust; he wrote on the same subject.] The exposure of Andromeda is told by Manilius, Ovid, and Pontanus; and the last did it best. Comparison of Vergil's Dido with the Ariadne of Catullus is followed by another *comparatio* without enlightening us as to the nature or the method of imitation. Rehearsal of literary forms (history, exposition, pleading) leads to the assertion that Cicero is the best model in all three styles.

III. Let us take Cicero, then, for our model. Proverbs, epigrams, definitions may be lifted as familiar enough to be common property. How to make variations on the model is exemplified abundantly in sentence form and in diction by both prose and verse. The book closes with many analyzed examples from Longueil, to rebut the charge that his writing is mere *cento,* or *pastiche,* and to exhibit him as the perfect Ciceronian. Ricci appends a practical hint from his own experience. His habit is to start boys with Terence because the plots are interesting, then to add some Cicero, and finally to give them Cicero alone.

The demonstration of Longueil's eloquence is rather an epilogue than a conclusion. It does not suffice to justify Ciceronianism, much less to explain imitation. The character of imitation, its limits, its profitable methods, are left still vague.

Of the same year is Bernardino Tomitano's *Discussions of Tuscan* (*Ragionamenti della lingua toscana* . . . Venice, 1545). The sub-title goes on: "wherein the talk is of the perfect vernacular orator and poet . . . divided into three books. In the first, philosophy is proved necessary to the acquisition of rhetoric and poetic; in the second are set forth the precepts of the orator; and in the third, the laws pertaining to the poet and to good writing in both prose and verse."

A dialogue in form, with an academy setting, this is largely a monologue by Speroni with interruptions, and is devoted mainly to "the perfect orator and poet." The book is a stilted and diffuse digest of conventional rhetoric jumbled with poetic, with examples under each conventional heading. Petrarch is made the exemplar of everything, even of argumentation. The idea of poetic as a distinct mode of composition never even enters.

I. Sperone Speroni, the protagonist, is made to repeat his contention that language study is not the gateway to philosophy and his epigram: "things make men wise; words make them seem so." Tomitano apparently takes him to mean that philosophy feeds style, not style philosophy; for Tomitano goes on to exhibit Petrarch as full of philosophy and perfect in style. Dante is less careful, but Petrarch is a treasury for all writers.

II. The anxiety to exhibit Petrarch leads to strange rendering of the conventional divisions of rhetoric. *Inventio,* "first of those five strings on which the orator makes smoothest harmony," is "imagining things that have truth, or at least verisimilitude," and is forthwith confused with *dispositio* (*compartimento*). Petrarch exemplifies not only *exordium* and *narratio,* but even proof and rebuttal. Of the "three styles" of oratory the highest is Boccaccio's in *Fiammetta,* the median in the *Decameron.* But since among verse forms the highest are *canzone, sestina,* and *madriale;* the plainest, *ballata, stanza,* and *capitolo;* the sonnet, Petrarch's favorite form, must be median. Under style the doctrine of "tone-color" is easily reduced to unintentional absurdity.

III. The distinction of poet from orator is discovered at great length to be—verse. The Ferrarese are best in comedies, the Venetians in sonnets, the Marchigiani in *capitoli,* they of Vicenza in *ballate,* the Romans in odes and hymns, the Paduans in tragedies, the Forentines in blank verse. *Inventio* in poetry is the rehearsal of myths, of which the poet is lord and guardian. An interruption! How can you put Petrarch above Dante when you began by urging that the poet should be a philosopher? Answer (240): Petrarch had all the philosophy he needed, and used it more poetically. Though Dante was the greater philosopher, Petrarch was the better poet. When Aristotle calls Sophocles more perfect than Euripides, he does not mean in style [!]. In poetry *dispositio* is evenness, consistency, harmony; and *narratio* has the same rules as in oratory. Horace's precepts, to begin *in mediis,* to combine instruction with charm, to seek advice, and to revise, are all repeated. On a request for more about style follows a discussion of words, simple and compound, proper and figurative, new and old. Finally the company joins in citing many examples.

Having run out of headings, Tomitano thus runs down. He had not in the least profited by the revival of Cicero and Quintilian.

Renaissance Platonism, disputing Aristotle's philosophy, attacked also his rhetoric. Francesco Patrizzi (1529–1597) published in his youth a collection of ten vernacular dialogues on rhetoric (*Della retorica, dieci dialoghi,* Venice, 1552), "in which," the sub-title adds, "the talk is of the art of oratory, with reasons impugning the opinion held of it by ancient writers." The Platonic dialogue, followed superficially, is quite beyond Patrizzi's achievement. Discussing oratory (I) at large, he goes on to its materials (II, III, IV), its ornaments (V), its divisions (VI), the quality of the orator (VII), the art of oratory (VIII), the perfect rhetoric (IX), and rhetorical amplification (X). Evidently neither a logical division nor a sequence, these categories are rather successive openings for attack. Patrizzi appears not only as a Platonist, but as an anti-Aristotelian. His main quarrels are with the scope of Aristotle's *Rhetoric,* with the doctrine of imitation, and with making rhetoric an art.

As to scope and materials Aristotle is inconsistent. He says both that the orator has no material and that he has all materials (25). Why, then, did he spend most of his *Rhetoric* on teaching the materials, slighting the ends, the ideas, the forms, the instruments, and omitting *status?* [The misinterpretation amounts to gross misstatement.] Perhaps we lack any clear definition of the orator because professors insist on including under a single word all sorts of discourse (27). Even the oratorical ornaments are not peculiar to the orator. His materials are the same as the economist's, the historian's, the poet's (37). Having given oratory so much scope, how can Aristotle restrict it to three kinds? (60). [Evidently superficial, this is rather quarrel and quibble than refutation.]

As to imitation, Patrizzi holds that a painter represents not his conception (*concetto*), but the objects themselves [a heresy that reappeared as lately as Ruskin's "pathetic fallacy"]. Taking no pains to understand what the Aristotelian imitation means, and ignoring the obvious fact that it is applied to poetic, he thus dismisses it by denial.

Similarly he finds that rhetoric is not an art because Plato says it is merely a skill (*peritia*).

The significance of this work is that in 1552 a Venetian seeking recognition at twenty-two could use some distinguished names in dialogues smartly rapping Aristotle, and even find a publisher.

The English rhetoric of Thomas Wilson (*The art of rhetorique, for the use of all such as are studious of eloquence, set forth in English,* London, 1553 [reprinted down to 1593; ed. G. H. Mair, Oxford, 1909]) covers the ancient scheme practically, using Cicero and Quintilian as well as the *Rhetorica ad Herennium,* and deriving much from Erasmus.

The *Partitiones oratoriae* (Venice and Paris, 1558) of Jacopo Brocardo is exactly described by its sub-title as *elegans et dilucida paraphrasis* of Aristotle's *Rhetoric.* Now translating, now paraphrasing, it provides in its marginal headings a sufficient table of contents.

But the revival of the full classical tradition is most obvious in the comprehensive Italian rhetoric of Bartolomeo Cavalcanti (*La retorica,* 1555; second edition, Venice, 1558/9, reprinted Pesaro, 1574). Through 563 closely printed pages this is strictly and consistently a rhetoric of the classical character and scope. The exceptional avoidance of confusion with poetic appears in the bare mention of Vergil and in the ousting of Petrarch from his monopoly as exemplar of everything desirable in prose as well as in verse. Plato is rare; Plutarch, rarer. The main body of analyzed examples is from the orations of Cicero. Demosthenes is only less frequent. From Livy and Thucydides the examples are usually of the imaginary harangues to troops. All the examples that are not themselves Italian are translated. Hermogenes is cited some half-dozen times; Quintilian, twice as often; but the main source of doctrine is the *Rhetoric* of Aristotle and, next to that, his Logic. The book is constantly and consistently Aristotelian.

Instead of devoting himself after the Renaissance habit mainly to style, Cavalcanti gives it only one of his seven books (V). All the rest are spent on composition. Book I is a lucid survey of the field; II shows the ways of *inventio* in each of the three types of oratory; III deals with argument; IV, with appeal to emotion and to moral habit; V, besides the usual lists of figures, has an unusually definite treatment of sentence management (*compositio*) and a meager summary of *dispositio;* VI presents the typical parts of an oration, avoiding the common confusion of *narratio* (statement of the facts) with narrative; VII deals with confirmation and conclusion. Its incidental recurrence to *dispositio* is again vague. Cavalcanti had excuse enough in the ancient tradition, which is generally weakest in its counsels for sequence.

Fortunately Cavalcanti's own plan is clear and fairly progressive; and his adjustment to his own time appears in the prominence given to the third of the ancient types of oratory, such speeches on occasion as were the main Renaissance field. His defect is the common Renaissance vice of diffuseness. Beyond its intrinsic value Cavalcanti's *Retorica* has historical significance. It gave the wider audience a just and distinct view of classical rhetoric.

The sixteenth century closed with the full classical doctrine operative in the *Ratio studiorum* and in the *Rhetoric* of Soarez.

Chapter IV

IMITATION IN LYRIC AND PASTORAL

THE lyrics of the fifteenth and sixteenth centuries show an extensive revival of Augustan measures in Latin. Meantime imitation of Petrarch made him an Italian classic and a European model. Thus, in England, revival from a meager and languid fifteenth century was stimulated in the sixteenth by Italy. But France shows the history of vernacular lyric in clearest stages: (1) in the formalizing of medieval modes by the *rhétoriqueurs;* (2) in the verse forms and diction of Lemaire and Marot, seeking variety without rejecting tradition; (3) in the Pléiade program of revolt from tradition to classicism, and especially in Ronsard's experiments with the Greek ode; (4) in the final predominance of the sonnet.

(a) Latin Lyric

Latin lyric was both changed in mode by the Renaissance and increased in volume. The fifteenth century turned from the modes of the medieval Latin lyric to more direct imitation of Vergil and Ovid, Catullus and Horace. Meantime the tradition of writing Latin verse in school continued to make every Renaissance author familiar with this metric. The difference was that he now used it in his own mature composition. For humanism demanded even of vernacular poets such Latin stanzas as might introduce the works of their friends, compliment their patrons, or celebrate state weddings, victories, and solemn entries. Though even published Latin lyrics were often themes, they at least promoted and confirmed two pervasive Renaissance literary habits: control of classical metric, and imitation. Throughout the Renaissance there is to be assumed in the back of a poet's mind a fund of classical measures and phrases.

But Renaissance Latin lyrics are by no means all themes. For some poets Latin was really the lyric medium. Humanistic anxiety and pretense about classical diction might, indeed, hinder lyric, but could not suppress it. Pontano (1426–1503), whose Latin poems fill nearly seven hundred modern pages, wrote not a few as directly and utterly lyrical as his *Naenia*. Jan Everaerts of Mechlin, known to literature as Secundus (1511–1536), even started a lyric vogue in Italy and France, and later in England, with his *Basia*. Obviously inspired by Catullus, they had a quality and influence of their own.

(b) *Italy and England*

The progress of vernacular lyric was steadiest in Italy because there the vernacular triumph had been recognized earliest and most consistently. The medieval lyric forms derived generically from Provençal—*canzone, ballata, sestina,* and *sonetto*—had all been explored by Dante; and one of them, the sonnet, had received from Petrarch a stamp that gave it European currency. Beside the humanist cult of Augustan Latin rose a cult of Petrarch as a vernacular classic. From Petrarch himself and through his fifteenth-century imitators the sonnet became the most widespread lyric mode both for a single, self-sufficient lyric and as a lyric unit in a narrative chain.

In England, where the range of medieval stanzas had been narrower, fifteenth-century lyric was meager. "The age of transition," as it has been called apologetically, was a period of medieval decadence, of stalling in medieval patterns. Without much stir of ideas, without general sureness in verse technic, it is often diffuse and straggling, as in Lydgate. Skelton's Latin learning remained quite apart from his slack and boisterous English verse; and English fifteenth-century lyric generally is both conventional and feeble. The sixteenth-century revival that was sought in Petrarch led here, as elsewhere, to the prevalence of sonnets. Its pioneer was Sir Thomas Wiat (1503– 1542). Starting with that connection of lyric with music which was to be a preoccupation of Ronsard, appreciating Chaucer, but reading him in imperfect texts, he turned early from a few *rondeaux* of the Marot type to the Petrarchan sonnet. Two thirds of his sonnets are translations or echoes of Petrarch himself, or are derived from his imitators. Wiat pursued Italian further in octaves and *terza rima* and seems to have read, besides Ariosto, Alamanni, Navagero, and Castiglione, the *Poetica* of Trissino (1529). The previous century had brought Italian influences on English learning; Wiat brought the first clearly literary influence since Boccaccio's on Chaucer. His friend Henry Howard, Earl of Surrey (1517–1547), carried this forward. Similarly following Petrarch and the Petrarchans, and experimenting with *terza rima* and other stanzas, he made Italian metric more familiar, and in particular helped to establish among the Elizabethans that form of sonnet which is called Shaksperian.

(c) France

France shows most distinctly the whole Renaissance lyric history. The beginning of the history in the medieval vernacular art of refrain stanzas had shown there the most systematic elaboration. In 1501 Antoine Vérard printed at Paris the huge collection of *balades, rondeaux,* and *virelais* entitled *Le jardin de plaisance et fleur de rhétorique. Rhétorique,* or more specifically *seconde rhétorique,* means the art of verse; the introduction expounds this in an anonymous treatise. Pierre Fabri incorporated the treatise in his *Grande et vraie art de pleine rhétorique* (Rouen, 1521). The *pleine* signifies merely the inclusion of both prose (Part I) and verse (Part II). Fullness in any other sense is hardly to be found in the *rhétoriques* of the period. They furnish mainly figures of speech and verse forms. They are style books; for the so-called school of the *rhétoriqueurs* was devoted mainly to verbal and metrical ingenuities.

But as Villon had shown in the early fifteenth century that the *balade* was not dead, so as the century waned Jean Lemaire (1473 to about 1520) was poet enough to be more than *rhétoriqueur.* True, he continued the jingling iteration. A double virelay composed on two rhymes begins as follows:

Hau*tains* es*prits* du grand royal pour*pris,*
Je suis *épris* par mouvements cer*tains*
De bien servir la reine de haut *prix.*
Mais trop sur*pris* est mon coeur malap*pris.* . . (p. 128).[1]

But Lemaire usually handled such recurrences with more delicacy.

Notre âge est bref comme les *fleurs*
Dont les cou*leurs* reluisent peu d'es*pace.*
Le temps est court et tout rempli de *pleurs*
Et de dou*leurs,* qui tout voit et com*passe.*
Joie se *passe;* on s'ébat, on so*lasse*
Et entre*lace* un peu de miel bénin
Avec l'amer du monde et le venin. . . (p. 17).

Using few of the popular medieval stanzas, he acknowledged Petrarch and Serafino d'Aquila (p. 238), composed the first part of his *Concorde des deux langages* in *terza rima,* and experimented with Alexandrines. The "enrichment" later proposed by Du Bellay he tried in such Latinisms as *aurein, calefaction, collocution, oscultation, congelative,* and *glandifère.* Bits of his pastoral decoration might have been written in the Pléiade.

A son venir Faunes l'ont adoré,
Satyres, Pans, Aegipans, dieux agrestes,
Et Sylvanus, par les bois honoré;

Nymphes aussi, diligentes et prestes,
A la déesse ont offert leur service,
Tout à l'entour faisant danses et festes.

Les Napées, exerçant leur office,
Font bouillonner fontaines argentines,
Créant un bruit à sommeil très propice.

[1] Paul Spaak, *Jean Lemaire* (Paris, 1926).

Puis à dresser les tentes célestines
Ont mis leur soin les mignonnes Dryades,
Faisant de bois ombrageuses courtines
(Concorde des deux langages, p. 243).

But the whole allegorical scheme of that poem is as medieval as Chaucer's in the *Parlement of Foules.* For Lemaire still uses mythology not for classical allusion, but medievally as an extension of allegory. Chaos and the Furies, Hymen, Erebus, Mercury, and Janus are listed (pp. 172–173) with the personifications Honor, Grace, Victory, and Discord. The medieval adaptation brings from the *Roman de la Rose* Bel-Accueil to be a sub-deacon in the temple of Venus (p. 252); for the temple, as in Chaucer, is a church and has relics. Even Hippolytus is a *"saint martyr"* (p. 223); and the three goddesses at the judgment of Paris are domesticated in Flanders by their *"venustes corpulences."* Jean Lemaire was not a forerunner of classicism.

Nor was Clement Marot (1495–1544). He learned the sonnet in Lyon and in Italy without discerning either its distinctive value or its future. For him it was merely one more form of the epigram type seen also in the *dizaine.* He continued the *balade,* adapted the *rondeau,* wrote much encomium without ever proclaiming himself a *vates.* His epistles, elegies, epigrams, his experiments with Alexandrines, his imitations of Martial, suggest a more normal development than the Pléiade change of both emphasis and direction.[2]

---

[2] Pierre Villey, *Les Grands Écrivains du xvi*e *siècle,* I, 83–97, 110–148.

For the new day of the sonnet at Lyon we must look to Louise Labé (about 1520–1566). Bourgeoise of the commercial and literary, French and Italian city of Lyon, composing sometimes in Italian and sometimes in French, she speaks the choice language of culture without parade. Her sonnets[3] are directly and utterly lyric. Their literary derivations may, indeed, be found, but are never put forward. Her few classical allusions are all familiar. The simple mythology of her prose *Débat de Folie et d'Amour* is handled in the Burgundian fashion of Jean Lemaire. Her verse is Petrarchan as it were inevitably, because that was the prevalent mode of her place and time. To call her a precursor of the Pléiade, then, may be quite misleading; for she suggests neither school nor date.

French humanism had still to attempt a stricter classicism, not adapting but imitating, not domesticating but importing. Ancient gods were to be recalled in the style of Vergil or of Ovid. Odes were to be Horatian, and might be Pindaric. Lyric diction was to be "enriched" by the interweaving of correct allusions in classical phrase. The allusive value would thus be heightened by summoning the hearer's culture to answer the poet's. Since poetry would be elevated by becoming learned, poets should be *docte*. As for readers insufficiently educated, they were not to be considered. Ronsard repeated Horace's *Odi profanum vulgus et arceo.* Let the poet seek "fit audience, though few." This whole theory of poetic allusion seems

---

[3] *Evvres de Louize Labé, Lionnoize,* revues et corrigées par la dite dame, à Lion, par Jean de Tournes, MDLVI (dedicatory epistle dated 1555).

to our age exploded. It comes to us through that standardized eighteenth-century poetic diction which was repudiated by the romantic revolt. Modern readers, consequently out of tune, must approach many Renaissance lyrics with a resolution of tolerance. Aurora leaving the bed of Tithonus, though mere decoration in Vergil and somewhat faded in the Middle Age, was not yet stale to the increasing audience of the sixteenth century. But if the allusion, far from being stale, were unfamiliar, even recondite? Instead of rejecting classical allusions *a priori* as hindrances to lyric, we may learn to estimate their value from actual Renaissance experience. That the language of poetry should be reminiscent of Greece and Rome was a Renaissance postulate.

Ronsard's early classicism, revolting from prolonged *rhétorique,* was reminiscent of Vergil and Ovid of course, of Catullus and his imitator Secundus, sometimes of Claudian and Pontano, but mainly of the Odes of Horace. Sometimes he even paraphrases, as when he composes a French *Fons Bandusiae;* often he adapts phrases; oftenest he follows the Horatian lyric movement. If he occasionally condescends to a medieval form, he gives it classical style. Further, his study of Greek under Dorat led him to imitate Callimachus and then Pindar. The reminiscences of Callimachus hardly go beyond the usual Renaissance lifting of phrase or allusion, that verbal classicism which was the habit of the time; but from Pindar he learned something different.

The extant poetry of Pindar is almost all encomium of victors at the pan-Hellenic contests. Encomium was a poetic fashion in the Renaissance too, because it was a means of publication. The Greeks had justified it by the poet's mission to confer fame. Though Ronsard adopts the idea in haughty proclamation of his own high function, he had already ancient warrant enough in Horace. What he learned further from Pindar was technical, a wider range of lyric composition. Encomium, reduced to recipe in late Greek oratory, took definite form earlier in Greek poetry. The main topics for the Pindaric celebration of an Olympian victor are his family line and his native city. Each of these is carried into legend and myth, either by allusions to what the pan-Hellenic audience knew as common tradition, or in the longer odes by verse narrative. The poem often ended on exhortation to live worthily of past and present fame. These conventional motives Pindar carried out metrically in a sequence of strophes and antistrophes. Without examining how strictly Ronsard followed the Greek mode, it is enough to say that his French adaptation proceeds by triads: strophe, antistrophe, epode. Though he usually followed Pindar's shorter odes, his Ode to the King on the Peace (1550) has ten triads; his Ode to Michel de l'Hospital (1550), twenty-four. In the latter the young Muses sing to Jupiter the battle of the Olympians with the Titans; and there follows an historical vision of the progress of poesy. Thus the Greek scheme invited Ronsard to wider adventures in metric, to more remote recurrences and larger lyric harmonies than were offered by Horace.

Though the metrical experiment ceased abruptly with Ronsard in 1550, it had later fruit in Spenser. Longer poems of occasion, thus introduced from the Greek by so skillful a metrist, were carried by the Pléiade influence to England. But Spenser's *Epithalamion* (1595) and *Prothalamion,* instead of conforming specifically to Ronsard's verse system, follow more generally and more variously the idea of larger metrical reach by framing a stanza of eighteen lines.[4]

Why did Ronsard drop such measures in 1550 at the age of twenty-seven? The Pindaric ode recurs sporadically in vernacular poetry, and occasionally has had a limited vogue. More or less Greek, it is often, as with Ronsard, learned and often pretentious with airs of inspiration. One of its rare successes came more than two centuries later in England with Gray. It has never kept its hold in lyric poetry. Ronsard continued to print his Pindarics among his collected poems; but he never again composed in those lyric modes. Had he found them intractable to his language or to his own bent? Having pushed allusiveness beyond the ken of any considerable audience, had he learned that lyric is remote at its peril? We may guess part of the answer from the times.

[4] Each stanza of the *Epithalamion* ends with a longer line (6 beats), which is the common refrain. The other lines have generally five beats, but the sixth and eleventh have only three; and this variation is occasionally extended. Generally there is a rhyme-shift after the eleventh line, but not a break (11 lines on 5 rhymes [or 4] plus 7 lines on 3 rhymes [or 4]). A few stanzas are lengthened to nineteen lines (11 plus 8). Thus the typical variations in this triumph of metrical interweaving are as follows, the underlined letters indicating the lines of three beats:

Stanza I. . . . . .a b a b c c b c b d d/ e f f e e g g
    II. . . . . .a b a b c c d c d f f/ g h h g g h h
    IV. . . . . .a b a b c c d c d e e/ f g g h h i i
    III. & VIII. . .a b a b c c d c d e e/ f g g f h h i i (19 lines)

Renaissance lyric thrived on learning so long as it was addressed to a special audience and sought reputation with patrons to whom learning might be useful in their dependents. The poet courtier naturally flattered princes or their ministers by assuming their familiarity with the classics as he displayed his own. But the printers had been widening the audience. Though 1550 was too early for what we now call a reading public, there was a widening circle, especially in the commercial cities, of readers who had some culture and desired more. Poets could begin to address these directly. Forty years later Spenser, still practicing encomium to win a position in which he could write, felt an English reading public and harmonized a long stanza without exhibiting Greek metric. Though Renaissance lyric remained largely aristocratic, even Ronsard, aristocrat himself, might find the mission of dispensing fame smaller than the opportunity of wider hearing.

For such wider appeal the readiest mode was the sonnet. Accepting Marot's scheme, Ronsard restricted his own practice to a few types especially suited to music. In thus using the new polyphonic art of voice with string accompaniment he applied the ancient idea of a sung lyric to the actual singing of his time. Modulating his many sonnets expertly, he showed equal control in other stanzas. That these familiar forms became a fitter pattern for Ronsard than the ode seems to us demonstrated by literary history. His Pindarics have been relegated to the museum; his more acclimated Horatian odes have been neglected; but time has not dimmed:

Quand vous serez bien vieille, au soir à la chandelle,
  Assise aupres du feu, deuidant & filant,
  Direz chantant mes vers, en vous esmerueillant,
  Ronsard me celebroit du temps que i'estois belle.
Lors vous n'aurez seruante oyant telle nouuelle,
  Desia sous le labeur à demy sommeillant,
  Qui au bruit de mon nom ne s'aille resueillant,
  Benissant vostre nom de louange immortelle.
Ie seray sous la terre & fantôme sans os
  Par les ombres myrteux ie prendray mon repos:
  Vous serez au fouyer vne vieille accroupie,
Regrettant mon amour & vostre fier desdain.
  Viuez, si m'en croyez, n'attendez à demain:
  Cueillez dés auiourdhuy les roses de la vie.[5]

Life is short; "gather ye roses while ye may"; the
theme is perennial, a lyric commonplace. The rendering of
it has often been conventional, but often, as here, individual because intensely realized. The sonnet is direct,
immediate, in renouncing all elaboration and all distrac-
tion. There are no allusions, only images. Candlelight,
hearth, loom, song, spoken words, are the sharper because
they are unmodified. There are few adjectives. The lyric is
simplified. But the images of attitude and gesture are
iterated to lead the mood: "assise auprès du feu, dévidant
et filant," "à demi sommeillant . . . réveillant," "accroupie." This is the diction of the lyrics that have no
date. For the point is not the abstract superiority of the
sonnet as a verse form; it is the appeal of form and diction
alike to a wider audience, the communication of poetry
rather than its exhibition. Ronsard shows this power of

[5] *Œuvres complètes de P. de Ronsard*, ed. par Paul Laumonier
(Paris, 1914–1919), I, 316.

direct appeal in his equally popular *Mignonne, allons voir si la rose.* Included in his first book of odes, this has no Greek strangeness. By 1550, having explored more remote modes to answer the special demand of his circle and his own bent toward learning, he returned to the lyric forms that had become familiar.

The sonnet sequence, the use of the sonnet as a lyric unit in a progress suggesting narrative, was more distinctly developed in England. Though Ronsard's sonnets appear in series, as addressed to Cassandre, Marie, or Hélène, the enchaining is more evident in Sidney's *Astrophel and Stella* and in Shakspere. Spenser, fully aware of the Pléiade, gave himself no such strict schooling as Ronsard's. He usually stopped short of ancient stanza and of borrowed phrase. But he relied longer on mythological allusions. Thus he decorated not only the *Faerie Queene,* but even his lyric triumph, the *Epithalamion.* Ronsard's later verse makes slighter and more considerate use of such ornament; Spenser's last poem still turns to the nymphs, to Jupiter and Leda, and to Hesper. The Renaissance lyric experience may be summed up in these two poets. Devoted to national revival of vernacular poetry, nourished by Latin and by Greek antiquity, expert metrists, they show together the limits of imitative classicism. Responding to the special demands of their time, they used the classics to certify their learning. Thus their lyric medium was surcharged. Its forms were sometimes so strange, its diction often so overloaded, as to sacrifice lyric directness, especially the immediate transmission of sensations. Lyric allusiveness was pushed be-

yond its lyric value. With lesser poets it often sufficed as
an end in itself. Renaissance "enrichment" often became
mere decorative dilation. But Ronsard, and then Spenser,
lived to fuse their experience of classicism in their appeal
to coming lovers of poetry.

2 . PASTORAL

Pastoral is an old dream. Classified by modern psy-
chology as escape, it has been in various forms the poetry
of the city wistful for the country. The word, denoting
shepherds, at the same time connotes that its shepherds
are not real, but fictitious. Whether allegorized or otherwise manipulated, they are not the actual men who
throughout history have tended beasts by day and night
in the open, not actual Sicilians, not even the shepherds
who in the Nativity plays brought English toys to the
infant Saviour. All these are real; the shepherds of
pastoral, wearing shepherd's clothes, sing other songs.
Artificial, indeed, pastoral has often been, and is easily,
but not always, not necessarily. The city dream of the
country "simple life" is after all a recurrent fact. Though
it may be sentimentalized, conventionalized, rhetoricated,
so may the other dreams. Instead of ruling out this one,
we may examine its literary vitality. Besides, it has a
special claim. Pastoral, ranging all the way from lyric
through narrative to dramatic, and from Alexandrian
Greek to Elizabethan English, offered in its Renaissance
vogue a wide school of imitation.

Renaissance taste in Greek inclined to that later literature called Alexandrian: to neo-Platonism, to the rhetoric

of Hermogenes, to Callimachus oftener than to Pindar, to the Byzantine imitators of Anacreon and the Byzantine Anthology of epigrams, to the descriptive show-pieces inserted in that late oratory called sophistic and in the "Greek Romances," both the long melodramas narrated by Apollonius, Heliodorus, and Tatius and the idyllic *Daphnis and Chloe* of that Longus who was called "the sophist." But the Renaissance literary creed for Latin was classicism. Inclined rather to the dilation of such later poets as Lucan, and even to Ausonius and Claudian, the Renaissance professed its faith in the artistic restraint of Vergil. Now pastoral had the promise of reconciling Alexandria with imperial Rome. It could turn for decoration both to the sophists and to Ovid. It was both Theocritus and Vergil.

The extant poems of Theocritus are by no means all pastoral. Called Idylls, that is little poems, they are love lyrics (II, III, XX); epigrams, that is, inscriptions of the sort collected in the *Anthology* (XXVIII and the following); myths (I in part, XI, XIII, XXIV–V); encomia (XIV in part, XVI–XVIII, XXII); and mimes, that is, dramatic dialogues (X, XV). Only seven of those that are surely his are such poetry-matches between shepherds as came to be called eclogues (I, IV–VII, X in part, XIV). Though this charming variety has suggested to modern critics hints for later pastoral development, especially toward drama, the vivacious realistic dialogue (XV) between two city women at the festival of Adonis is essentially different from pastoral. Nor is it true to either poet to say that pastoral with Theocritus was fresh and natural; with Vergil it became artificial. Both poets knew the country, Vergil apparently better than Theocritus; but neither gives it that direct, immediate expression which in modern times has been called nature poetry. Theocritus is specific with wild olive, peas, and acorns; sometimes concrete with a smoky hen-roost, waving green leaves, or a crested lark. For an Alexandrian he is exceptionally free from the dilation of descriptive showpieces; but he has the Alexandrian habit of seeing nature through art. Gorgo and Praxinoa (XV) are conveyed by their chatter; and the dirge to Adonis describes the *putti* on the ceremonial coverlet as like fledgling nightingales trying their wings. Sicily is romantic for us with blue sea, wild uplands, and volcanic steeps. The shepherds of Theocritus live nearer to sophisticated Syracuse or Agrigentum, or to the other western cities of ancient Greece. Unlike enough otherwise, Theocritus and Vergil are alike in viewing the country through the eyes of the city.

The *Bucolics* of Vergil established pastoral in its most familiar pattern. One of the few schoolbooks to hold their place from ancient into modern times, they have drilled into successive thousands the poetic scheme of a lyric contest for some rustic prize, and the idea that this contest, symbolizing some other more momentous, may express the poet's own hopes and fears. Thus in school, as from time immemorial boys got their first notions of wordly wisdom by memorizing Latin beast-fables, so they learned Latin grammar, with Latin verse, from shepherd rivalries typifying wider struggles. Since many Renaissance boys continued to imitate the *Bucolics* when they grew up, many Renaissance eclogues are published themes. That Vergil's eclogues have survived all this is evidence of immortality. They need no further praise; but having been used for grammar, they need to be read again for poetry and for literary history.

The inspiration of Theocritus, gracefully acknowledged by Vergil (IV, VI, X), is hardly of style. The avoidance of descriptive dilation, the preference of specific indication to ornament, are Vergil's own choice.

Pauperis et tuguri congestum caespite culmen (I. 69)

More characteristic of his economy is his use of concrete predicates.

> Molli paulatim flavescet campus arista,
> Incultisque rubens pendebit sentibus uva;
> Et durae quercus sudabunt roscida mella (IV. 28).

More concise than Theocritus in style, and graver, he is quite independent in composition. The *Pharmaceutria* (VIII) owes to the second idyll of Theocritus little but the subject. The encomium of *Pollio* (IV), instead of following the sophistic recipe item by item, selects and weaves into an integrated vision of the Golden Age. But such economy of phrase and movement seems to have had less influence in making his eclogues models than his use of shepherd rivalries to suggest larger struggles and personal concerns.

Moralized eclogue was familiar from the schoolbook called *Auctores octo*. As used at Troyes in 1436, this collection contained, with an *Isopet* (Aesop's fables), a *Cathonet* (maxims of Cato), and other medieval com-pends, a *Théodolet.* The work thus familiarly styled is *Theodulus* (or *Liber Theoduli*), *ecloga qua comparantur miracula Veteris Testamenti cum veterum poetarum commentis.* It matches pagan with Christian instances in a contest of Falsehood (Pseustis) with Truth (Alethia) which is judged by Reason (Phronesis) Probably of the ninth century, it was printed as late as the sixteenth.[6] Literary use of Latin eclogues during the intervening centuries is sufficiently indicated by Dante's in reply to Giovanni di Virgilio. Petrarch's Vergilian *Bucolicum carmen* expresses the actual conflict of Christian with pagan poetry. Boccaccio's eclogues are less distinctive than his Italian prose narrative *Ameto.* Though this is far longer than any previous pastoral and is dilated with lavish description, it must be remembered not only for its pastoral setting, but for its alternations of verse and for its myth. The successive interviews of the shepherd with the nymphs and demigoddesses symbolize the progress from earthly to heavenly love.[7]

But humanism must have its own eclogues and its own symbolism. The eclogues (1498) of Mantuan (Baptista Spagnolo, known as Mantuanus, 1448–1513) were lifted out of the humanist throng by being adopted for use in school. The imitation thus invited through some two hundred years was the easier because they are far less concise than Vergil's. Vicar General of the Carmelites, Mantuan doubtless owed some of his vogue to his

---

[6] London, Wynkyn de Worde, 1515.
[7] For Petrarch and Boccaccio, see Carrara, *La poesia pastorale,* pp. 88–111.

edification. Nevertheless he admits that classicizing which Erasmus attacked later as paganizing: *Tonans,* for instance, or *Regnator Olympi* for God. Eclogue III presents the convention of hopeless, ill-starred love; IX, the conventional contrast of country to city; but X makes the shepherds debate the actual controversy over the Observantists. Eclogue IV finds women still, as of old, *servile genus, crudele, superbum.* Most of its examples being classical, boys could learn simultaneously to recognize allusions and to beware women. Mantuan occasionally indulges in word-play.

> invida res amor est, res invidiosa voluptas (II. 167).

> Nescio quis ventos tempestatesque gubernat;
> id scio (sed neque si scio, sat scio, sed tamen ausim
> dicere—quid?) (III. 12–14).

> his igitur quae scire nefas nescire necesse est
> posthabitis (III. 41–42).

He may overlook an awkward internal rhyme.

> quae mea *sit* me cog*it* amor sententia fari
> liberaque ora fac*it* (II. 160–61).

But generally he is as accomplished in ease as in classicism.

Six years after Mantuan's collection, another Italian writer of Latin eclogues, Jacopo Sannazaro (1458–1530), published a vernacular pastoral, *Arcadia* (1504),[8] so widely popular as to become almost the sixteenth-century type. Though the name is Greek, Arcadia and Arcadian have been ever since reminiscent of Sannazaro. Through

---

[8] Edited by M. Scherillo (Torino, 1888).

him, more than through any other single influence, vernacular pastoral spread over western Europe. For he gathered up in prose narrative with verse interludes most of what pastoral in its long history had become. Saturated in Vergil, familiar among the other Latin poets and with Greek, he had caught the possibilities of Boccaccio's *Ameto;* and though he weaves throughout from literature, never directly from life, he was artist enough to weave originally. The *Arcadia* shows Renaissance imitation at its best.

Apter most often to attract the eye are the tall and spreading trees reared by nature on rugged mountains than the cultivated plants pruned by expert hands in decorative gardens; and much apter to please the ear the wild birds singing on green branches amid solitary thickets than among city crowds the trained ones in winsome and decorated cages. For which reason the woodland songs, too, methinks, inscribed in the stiff bark of beeches no less delight the reader than the choice verses written on the fair pages of illuminated volumes; and the waxed reeds of the shepherds in their flowery valleys offer perchance a pleasanter sound than the polished and vaunted instruments of the musicians in halls of ceremony. And who doubts that more attractive to human minds is a fountain springing naturally from the living rock, surrounded by green herbage, than all the others made by art of whitest marble resplendent with gold? Surely, as I believe, no one. Relying, therefore, on this, I may well on these deserted slopes, to the listening trees and to such few shepherds as may be there, tell the rude eclogues springing from the vein of nature, leaving them as bare of ornament as I heard them sung by the shepherds of Arcadia to the liquid murmur of their fountains. For to these not once, but a thousand times, the mountain gods, won by their sweetness, gave attentive ear; and the tender nymphs, forgetting to chase their wandering prey, left their quivers and bows beneath the lofty pines of Menalus and Lycus. Whence I, if I may, would rather have the glory of putting my lips to the humble reed of Corydon, given him long ago by Dametas as a precious gift, than to the resounding clarinet of Pallas, with which the presumptuous satyr challengened Apollo to his own destruction. For surely it is better to cultivate well a little plot than to leave a great one by ill management foully crowded with stubble.

There lies toward the summit of Parthenio, no mean mountain of shepherd Arcadia, a delectable plain, not very ample in size, being bounded by the build of the place, but so full of fine and greenest herbage that only the sportive flocks, feeding there greedily, hinder perpetual verdure. [Follows a list of its trees, with appropriate adjectives and allusions. In spring, when the glade is at its best, shepherds meet there to match their skill with lance or bow, with leap and rustic song. At such a time Ergasto, moping apart, was challenged by Selvaggio in *terza rima*.]

Such are the prelude to *Arcadia* and its first eclogue; and so it continues. For the whole book is an alternating series of prose descriptions and lyrics. There is no narrative sequence and arrival. We are bidden to linger in Arcadia, to move only from one grouping to another. The alternation of prose and verse, as old as Boethius, was new for pastoral. For its time the fluent rhythmic prose, at once easy and regulated, was the distinctive achievement. The verse is competent in a considerable range of meters. Both prose and verse, whether in reminiscence of pastoral hexameters or in feeling for a rhythm natural to Italian speech, are largely dactylic. Meter XII ends with a dactyl every one of its 325 lines; but Sannazaro's habit is no such *tour de force*. His dactyls are not insistent; they are merely predominant in a pleasant variety. For he is studious of variation. In the first eclogue Ergasto's reply links some ten tercets by internal rhyme (lines 61–91):

> Menando un giorno l'agni presso un fi*ume,*
> Viddi un bel l*ume* in mezzo di quell'*onde,*
> Che con due bi*onde* trezze allor me str*inse,*
> Et me dip*inse* un volto in mezzo al c*ore,*
> Che di col*ore* avanza lacte e r*ose;*
> Poy si nasc*ose* immodo dentro all'*alma,*
> Che d'altra s*alma* non me aggrava il peso.

and then resumes the *terza rima*. In Meter II, lines 86–96, the responses begin by repeating the rival's last line, somewhat as in the refrains of popular poetry. Sannazaro is a careful artist.

The diction achieves a pretty balance between ease and suggestiveness. Easy with conventionally appropriate adjectives and fluent cadences, it is full of echoes. At once we are reminded of Vergil, soon of Ovid, Horace, Theocritus, Catullus, and also of their imitators. The great range of this appropriation can be measured by the crowded footnotes of the commentators; but without measuring, sometimes without distinct recognition, we hear a constant accompaniment. Renaissance allusiveness, too often paraded, is here subdued to serve the pastoral mood. Vergil was in this glade. Theocritus set such a jar for the rustic prize. This myth is prettiest in Ovid. But though an allusion lurks under every bush, it will not leap out to detain us. Whatever pastoral poets we know help to make us yield ourselves with at least a wistful "Et ego in Arcadia vixi." Tasso, indeed, was to outdo him with *Aminta;* but the difference is in degree, not in method. In 1504 Sannazaro succeeded at the Renaissance task of making literature out of literature.

Dramatic pastoral was one of the forms of Renaissance pageantry. It put shepherds, nymphs, and satyrs on the stage to enhance the celebration of court festivity with scenic device and music. It gave mythology representation without changing the pastoral type.

Though carefully limited in time to secure consecutive action, Tasso's *Aminta*[9] is much less dramatic than pastoral. It weaves within the dramatic frame the pastoral tissue of wistful reminiscence. It revives the ancient dream of the Golden Age, not only through scenery and the music of instruments and of verse, but by constant allusiveness of style.

Within twenty-five pages Solerti's notes record echoes of Sappho, Theocritus, and Achilles Tatius; of Lucretius, Vergil (oftenest), Horace, Catullus, Tibullus, Propertius, Ovid, Seneca, Claudian, Statius, Nemesianus, Calpurnius, Cornelius Gallus; of Dante, Petrarch (oftenest), Boccaccio, Poliziano, Sannazaro, Bembo—but why go on? Even so heavy a charge of reminiscence is managed without overloading. The *Aminta* is the most consistent, as it is perhaps the most accomplished, example of this form of Renaissance borrowing. Tasso makes discreet use of alliteration and of word-play. His musical verse should be

[9] Written 1573; published 1580; edited by Angelo Solerti (Torino, 1901).

heard, not merely read. The pervasive harmony, various and subtle, can be but suggested by underlining a few recurrences in the opening scene.

> L'acqua e le ghiande ed or l'acqua e le ghiande,
> Sono cibo e bevanda.
>
> Che tu dimandi amante ed io nemico
> La vita s'avviticchia a'l suo marito.

The delicate weaving of sound and sense, allusion and image, has not faded. Few works of the Renaissance have had more modern admirers than the *Aminta*.

The continuance of the type and the spread of its vogue appear in the twelve eclogues of the *Shepherds' Calendar* (1579). Spenser turned to it as to the established European form in which to prove oneself classical and offer one's poetic encomium. It was the obvious medium by which to win rank as a poet. But at once appears a marked difference. Instead or relying on the pastoral fund of allusion, Spenser provides an apparatus of explanation: a dedicatory epistle, a general argument for the whole series, a prefatory argument for each eclogue, and a gloss. The last explains even obvious classical allusions, interprets the allegory, indicates that this phrase is taken from Theocritus and that from Vergil, and sometimes adds learned references. Did English readers need all this? The answer is not that Sidney, Leicester, Raleigh, Burleigh, Elizabeth herself, had not read Vergil and Mantuan, but rather that Spenser, even while he must still depend for a living on the court, was conscious of a wider audience. There were already English lovers of poetry, and there were soon to be more, who, having less culture than they desired, were glad to be guided in Arcadia.

The gloss also supports Spenser's attempt to make his pastoral English. It explains his deliberate archaism; for he tries to recall the language of Chaucer without quite understanding it himself. Though of course he caught Chaucer's drift, he did not always catch his rhythms, nor even his grammar. Archaism, dubious enough in itself, is thus doubly dubious here. The diction of pastoral has an added strangeness. Sidney deplored this in his *Defense of Poesy:* "That same framing of his stile to an old rustick language I dare not alowe, sith neyther *Theocritus* in Greeke, *Virgill* in Latine, nor Sanazar in Italian did affect it." Ben Jonson's dismissal may be blunt; but it is precise: "Spenser in affecting the ancients writ no language." If such diction may occasionally suggest actual country speech, it is but the farther removed from the pastoral mood.

Spenser's eclogues are English also in their nationalist fear and scorn of Rome. Cultivated by government policy, this was so widespread as to assure him a response. Moreover pastoral had always expressed controversies beyond shepherds. But pastoral allegory has been most acceptable when it is least local. Mantuan's Observantist discussion and Spenser's "Papists" have long been tedious. We might look them up in the footnotes, if they did not seem too remote from the concerns of the Golden Age. For pastoral at its best is not English, nor French, nor Italian; it is Arcadian, translatable readily into any language because it has no country. Its allusiveness breaks down when it sends us to a guidebook.

Otherwise Spenser's eclogues are not distinctive. Their verbal mythology is discreetly limited to familiar deities; their imitation, except for one paraphrase of Marot, is of the usual authors; their pattern is the Vergilian type. If the April encomium of Elizabeth is fulsome, that was the habit of her court. If the metric is sometimes disappointing with crowded stresses, or padded rhymes, or even jingle, that is because Spenser was experimenting. The significance of the *Shepherds' Calendar* is not its pastoral achievement, but its use of the mode to win recognition and its attempt to push pastoral farther than it would go.

In spite of its pastoral title, Sir Philip Sidney's *Arcadia* (c. 1583) has a different pattern. Though it has incidental pastoral, its design is that of the long, loose, complicated, melodramatic tales of Alexandria known as the Greek Romances. These decadent Greek prose stories had wide circulation in the Renaissance; and one, the *Daphnis and Chloe,* is both better organized than most of them and clearly reminiscent of pastoral. Since its vogue was increased by the French translation of Amyot, it may be counted among Renaissance pastoral influences. For pastoral has appeared again and again not as the main intention of a whole work, but as an incidental interest. Though Renaissance imitation was thus sometimes of style, sometimes merely of decoration, it was also quite clearly the study of an ancient literary form.

Chapter V

ROMANCE

SIXTEENTH-CENTURY poetic has no specific relation to Renaissance development of verse narrative.
The more pervasive counsels and habits of imitation agree
in exalting Vergil. Vergil did, indeed, guide the narrative
sequence of Tasso; but narrative sequence is not a general
Renaissance concern. Malory, Boiardo, Ariosto, Spenser,
seek other narrative values. What they have in common
preoccupation and common achievement is romance.
Romance in a period of classicism, romance written in
spite of humanism and sometimes by humanists—what
should it be? It was response to the special audience of
the courts; for, whatever humanism might say, the courts
liked romances. It was response also to the wider audience
steadily increased by printing. The response, both in
medieval continuance and in distinctive Renaissance
direction, constitutes an important chapter in literary
history.

I. THE ROMANTIC CONTRAST

The good old times recreated by poetry for refuge and
inspiration were found by Malory and Spenser at the
court of Arthur; by the Italian romancers, at the court of
Charlemagne. These, of course, are the two main medieval
fields of romance, *matière de Bretagne* and *matière du roi;*
and into either of them may enter incidentally the matter

of Troy with the progeny of Aeneas or "Hector's arms."
Though the Charlemagne tradition may be somewhat
more distinct with its twelve paladins and its one traitor,
the two are essentially alike in being, for the actual
world out of joint, kingdoms of chivalry. Thither the
Renaissance turned from the Wars of the Roses or the
hired soldiers of Italy. Gunpowder had abolished single
combat; feudalism was gone; chivalry had been reduced
to ceremony. Therefore romance was out of date. No; the
fact that romance survived the Renaissance shows that it
has no date. The romantic *therefore* is that poetry must
once more revive ideals. Sinister violence in Warwickshire
or Ferrara denies chivalry; romance revives it.

This fundamental motive strikingly unites the two
fifteenth-century soldier romancers Malory and Boiardo.

Sir Thomas Malory (1394?–1471) was attached in his
young manhood to the retinue of the great Richard Beau-
champ, Earl of Warwick, widely celebrated as a pattern of
chivalry. After much military service he sat in the Parliament
of 1445. Arraigned in 1451 before a local court at Nuneaton
on the charge of breaking into the abbey of St Mary at
Coombe and robbing it, and further of ambushing the Duke
of Buckingham, he was remanded to the King's Bench and
imprisoned for most of his last twenty years. In Newgate
Jail he finished his *Morte d'Arthur* (1469–1470). These few
facts, opening much inference, tell us surely that he was imprisoned for violence in a time of violence. The chivalry that
he celebrates in the greatest English literary work of a sterile
period has the relief of contrast.

Matteo Maria Boiardo (1434–1494), usually called "the
Count," was brought up at the brilliant ducal court of Ferrara.
He was sent on embassies, married a Gonzaga, was gentleman

of honor to Eleonora, and governor (*Capitano*), first (1480) of Modena, and then (1487, the year in which he published the first two books of his *Orlando innamorato*) of Reggio. Tradition has him genial and easy-going, and adds picturesquely that when he found a sonorous name for one of his Carolingian heroes he volleyed his castle bells.

His writing was abundant, various, characteristic of his time: ten Latin eclogues and several Latin epigrams; many Petrarchan sonnets, with *canzoni* and madrigals; ten Italian eclogues; *capitoli* on fear, jealousy, hope, love, and excellence (*virtù*); a five-act comedy, *Timone*, drawn from Lucian; translations from Herodotus, Xenophon's *Cyropaedia*, the *Golden Ass* of Apuleius, and the *Lives* of Cornelius Nepos.

Different enough in fortune, the two had the same experience of actual war, and turned from it with the same literary motive, a wistful and generous desire to animate the dislocated and groping present with the courage and devotion of an idealized great past. Poetry of escape, this is also poetry of faith. It lifts Symphorien Champier's clumsy *Gestes ensemble la vie du preulx chevalier Bayard* (1525) with the ideal of a knight "sans peur et sans reproche." It will seize upon the death of Sir Philip Sidney as romantic. It will survive the allegorizing of Spenser. It is the refuge from the industrial age in Tennyson's *Idylls of the King*. If fighting and politics remain as ugly as in the fifteenth century, Edwin Arlington Robinson will not be the last poet of romance.

Boiardo makes the contrast very explicit.

[The robber replied] "What I am doing every great lord does in your upper world. They make havoc of their enemies in war for aggrandizement and to cut a bigger figure. A single man like me makes trouble for seven, perhaps ten; they rage against ten thousand. And they do still worse than I in that they take what they do not need." [Said Brandimarte] "It is indeed a sin to take from one's neighbor as my world does; but when it is done only for the state, it is not evil; it is at least pardonable." [The robber replied] "A man is more easily pardoned when he frames the charge himself. And I tell you, and make full confession, that I take what I can from any one who can less" (II. xix. 40).

O Fame, attendant of emperors, nymph so singing great deeds in sweet verse that thou bringest men honor even after death and makest them eternal, where art thou fallen? To sing ancient loves and tell the battles of giants. For the world of this thy time cares no longer for fame or for excellence (II. xxii. 2).

Then with choice rhymes and better verse shall I make combats and loves all of fire. Not always shall the time be so out of joint as to drag my mind from its seat. But now my songs are lost. Of little avail to give them a thought while I feel Italy so full of woe that I cannot sing, and hardly can I sigh. To you, light lovers and damsels, who have at heart your noble loves, are written these fair stories flowering from courtesy and valor. They are not heard by those fell souls who make their wars for despite and rage (II. xxxi. 49–50).

The distinctive difference between the two fifteenth-century romancers is that Malory translates; Boiardo rewrites. Malory may contract or expand, adapt or add; but in general he follows what he calls "the French book." Boiardo, finding the Italian versions vulgarized (*tra villani,* II. xii. 3), wishes to make the old tradition once more literary. To restore their dignity, he gives the paladins more than verse. So romance throughout the

Renaissance, as before and since, both survived and was changed. It was rehearsed, translated, printed in its medieval forms; and it was shaped to a distinctive Renaissance pattern.

2. SEPARATE ROMANCES

What the presses most readily carried on from the Middle Age was the separate romances that had not been merged in one of the cycles. The old fairy-mistress story told by Jean d'Arras as *Mélusine* (1387) was printed at Geneva in 1468. *Pontus and the Fair Sidoine,* translated into German in 1468, was printed in French at Lyon in 1484 and in German at Augsburg in 1548. *Amadis of Gaul* traveled from Brittany to Spain and Portugal and back to France. The French prose version printed in 1540 and again in 1548,[1] typically romantic in love, adventure, and chivalry, deserved its popularity also by narrative skill. With some lyric dilation of love and an occasional allusion to classical mythology, the style is generally restrained to the narrative purpose. Description, rarely dilated, is often cleverly inwoven. Dialogue adds not only liveliness, but some characterization. Though the simple transitions sound like Malory's ("Now the author leaves this and returns to the treatment of the child"), this shifting is not frequent; often it does not really interrupt; and generally the composition has distinct narrative sequence. The knighting of Amadis is not merely a scene in a series; it is a situation, prepared and pointed as at once

[1] *Le Premier Livre d'Amadis de Gaule,* publié sur l'édition originale par Hugues Vaganay (Paris, 1918), 2 vols.

fulfillment and promise. So the complication of the rings (Chapter XI) is carried out before our eyes through suspense to solution.

In such separate romances the Middle Age had advanced the art of verse narrative. Not only in Chaucer's masterpiece *Troilus and Criseyde,* but also in the contemporary *Gawain and the Green Knight,* the story is carried forward in consistent sequence to a distinct issue of character. The Renaissance, though generally it had other preoccupations, caught some of this vigor in the telling of single romances. One of these, loosely related to the Arthurian cycle without ever being embodied, is of Giron; and this was put into Italian stanzas by Luigi Alamanni (1495–1556). An industrious and capable man of letters,[2] who spent much of his life in France, he was a convinced classicist. His *Gyrone il cortese* (Paris, 1548; Venice, 1549), though it was written long after Ariosto had secured fame by quite other methods, shows that he felt the obligation of a single story, distinct from a cycle, to keep narrative sequence.

Alamanni's Dedicatory Epistle, after relating the Arthur stories to history, and mentioning some dozen of the Arthurian heroes, expounds tournaments and the quests of errant knights, and offers his Gyrone, as Caxton offers his Malory, to educate toward true valor. Confessing that he has not always followed his source in detail, he promises later "another new work of poetry . . . made in the ancient style and order and imitating Homer and Vergil." [This was fulfilled in the last years of his life by his *Avarchide.*]

[2] For Alamanni, see Henri Hauvette, *Un Exilé florentin . . .* Luigi Alamanni (Paris, 1903).

The first five books proceed as follows. After preliminary adventures, Gyrone goes to his bosom friend Danain at Malahalto. On news of a tournament they decide to go disguised in black arms (II). But Danain's wife languishes for love of Gyrone and gains permission to go thither also under escort while the two friends lodge with a hermit. After combats on the way, they arrive at the tournament as Sagramor is victorious in the first jousts. The beauty of Danain's wife arouses the jealousy of the other ladies and the passion of the Greek king Laco. His ardor and his threats to seize her are overheard by Gyrone, who courteously rebukes him in a lecture.

Further description of the combats at the tournament (III) leads to the final victory of Gyrone and Danain. While Laco still yearns (IV) toward Danain's wife, a messenger arrives to conduct her to a neighboring castle. Laco parts from Meliadus, as Gyrone from Danain. Thus Laco and Gyrone are left sighing for the same lady in the same forest. They meet, express their admiration of each other, and sleep side by side in the wood.

In the morning Laco routs single-handed the lady's whole escort (V). The lady appealing eloquently to his honor in vain, Gyrone arrives and fells him. While the lady debates with herself whether to reveal her love, and Gyrone is torn by the conflict of his own with his loyalty to Danain, they are irresistibly drawn together. In a flowery mead by a spring they prepare for love. But Gyrone's lance falling knocks his sword into the spring. When he has retrieved it, he reads as never before its inscription summoning to honor, and turns it in shame on himself. A peasant supervening betrays their sad plight to Laco.

Thus the story is brought definitely to a situation of character. Obvious as the Renaissance manipulation is in the space given to love, the handling makes this not merely lyric interlude, but story motive. Though Alamanni is unwilling, or unable, to carry this through the 28,000 lines of his twenty-four books, though he often fails to give that salience to critical situations which is evident here, he nevertheless achieves what the Renaissance cyclical romances generally ignored, narrative sequence. All he needed to make his *Gyrone* shorter, tighter, more compelling, was firmer control of fourteenth-century narrative art.

For a classicist Alamanni is remarkably sparing of the fashionable Renaissance allusions. He does, indeed, use that paganizing phrase which was satirized by Erasmus. "In the consecrated temples, devoutly about the sacrifices in accordance with true example, they listened, adored, and besought the immortal Father"; when Malory would say, "They heard their Mass and brake their fast." But in spite of many Vergilian similes and of occasional orations to troops, Alamanni's classicism is not intrusive. Apparently he thought it had small place in romance.

3. THE ARTHURIAN CYCLE IN MALORY

Among Renaissance romances presenting a traditional cycle in medieval form the most distinguished is Malory's *Morte d'Arthur*. Caxton's preface is a manifesto of romance; and his table of contents displays most of the stories that had gradually been brought together by the Middle Age at the Round Table. Between the *"enfances"* of the first book and the last great battle in the west are Balin and Tristan; that Percival, here called Gareth or Beaumains, who was reared apart in the wildwood; the mighty Lancelot, his mistress the Queen, and Elaine who

died for love of him; the quest of the Grail; the traitor
Modred. They are not composed in a narrative sequence.
Balin, Gareth, Tristan, for instance, remain separate
stories. For there is no real connection in Balin's glimpse
of an earlier Grail story not used in Malory's Grail books,
or in Gareth's coming to Camelot and his knighting by
Lancelot. But there is no confusion. The separate stories
are told straightforwardly; the main persons become
familiar; and the exposure of Guinevere makes a crisis
contributing to the subsequent ruin of the goodly fellow-
ship. The *Morte d'Arthur* is not merely a series. But its
distinction is in style. Malory's prose follows that medieval habit which may be called pure narrative, the telling
of a story singly for its story values. It was not the only
medieval narrative habit; nor is he the only fifteenth-
century author to follow it; but it stands out both in contrast to classicism conceived as ornamental dilation and in
his own quiet mastery. Without parade, without pause for
ornament, he maintains a grave simplicity that ranges
from homeliness to eloquence. His rhythm—he has little
other sentence art—lingers or quickens with the action,
and answers the emotion.

Is that knyght that oweth this shelde your love? Yea truly,
said she, my love he is. God wold I were his love (XVIII.
xiv).

Than syr Bedwere cryed: "Ah! my lord Arthur, what shal
become of me now ye go from me and leve me here allone
emonge myn enemyes?" "Comfort thy self," sayd the kyng,
"and doo as wel as thou mayst; for in me is no truste for to
truste in. For I wyl in to the vale of Avylyon to hele me of
my grevous wounde" (XXI. v).

4. THE CAROLINGIAN CYCLE
ON THE STREET

The other cycle, the Carolingian, was popularized in Italy by street story-tellers, who seem to have been, on the piazza before audiences of artisans and shopkeepers, somewhat like the medieval *jongleurs* before their successive groups of pilgrims. Their narrative art can be only guessed; for it was oral. But the guess is helped by the persistence, even to the present time, of the Carlomagno marionettes. The recital animated by these large puppets—for it is recital, not drama—is of a traditional version called *I paladini di Francia,* and goes on day after day by mere aggregation, and with many tirades.

5. PULCI

Italian literary manipulation of the Carolingian cycle in verse romances began with Luigi Pulci (1432–1484). His *Morgante maggiore* (1481, though largely written by 1470)[3] is selective. Though it bulks large with more than 30,000 lines of verse, it does not rehearse the deeds of the paladins by the serial method of installments. At the end of Canto 5 two main stories, Orlando's and Rinaldo's, are brought together. At the end of Canto IX, having meantime moved together, the two arrive, with the other persons whom they have picked up on the way, for the relief of Montauban and of Carlomagno at Paris. There is narrative progress from salience to salience. The dialogue is lively. Though it does not amount to characterization, it suffices for speed and for mood.

[3] Edited by G. B. Weston (Bari, 2 vols.).

Said Rinaldo, "Wilt thou be so obtuse as not to look at that damsel? Thou wouldst not be acceptable as a lover. . ." Said Oliver, "Thou art ever for thy jokes. Yonder is something more serious than word-play" (IV. 61).

Oliver looked at Rinaldo, hardly able to hold his gaze for weeping, and said: " 'Tis true that man cannot hide love and coughing. As thou seest, dear brother, love has caught me at last with his claws. I can no longer hide this desire. I know not what to do, what to decide. Cursed be the day on which I saw her. What am I to do? What dost thou advise?" Said Rinaldo, "Believe me, thou wilt leave this place. Leave the lady, marquis Oliver. Our intention was not to yearn, but to find Orlando" (IV. 88–90).

The naughty machinations of Malagigi are, indeed, comic interpolations; nothing comes of them; but the machinations of Gano have narrative function. There is hardly any separable description. Love laments are sketched, not dilated. Pulci is interested, and interests us, in his story as a story. To this end he takes a free hand with events. We have the usual paynim siege of Paris or of Montauban, but no attempt to include all the items of tradition. Pulci takes what he wishes and puts it where he wishes.

To call the poem a burlesque is misleading. The in-cidental farce, as in Boiardo and Ariosto, is rather appeal to Renaissance fondness for the grotesque as contrast. Though Pulci may have wished to pierce the inflation of the Carolingian street tirades, he was too clever to think of holding parody through 30,000 lines. Reducing the medieval aggregation to an intelligible story, he also, with an art more delicate than burlesque, reduced the style. Turning from both medieval gravity and Renaissance luster, he brought romance down to earth. Oliver falls in love promptly, utterly, and successively. The humor of this in real life Pulci frankly seeks. When two knights dare each other, he renders their speech not as oration, but as homely flyting. He is irreverent in the way of fashionable conversation. But his main object and achievement, as it is not parody, so it is not satire. It is pleasant, often humorous story of familiar antiquated persons in traditional events and setting, but in daylight.

6. BOIARDO

Boiardo, indignant at the degradation of the Carolingian heroes among the vulgar—how did he proceed toward elevation?

Who will give me the voice and the words, and utterance magnanimous and profound? (I. xxvii. 1).

Till now my song has not ventured far from shore. Now I must enter upon the great deep, to open immeasurable war. All Africa lies beyond that sea; and all the world flashes with men in arms (II. xvii. 2).

The poet seems to nerve himself, as Vergil at the opening of *Aeneid* VII, for loftier diction. The average Renaissance poet of the next century would invoke the Muses for that "high style" which had come down from classical through medieval rhetoric. But the words of Boiardo's invocation are not heightened thus; nor is his diction generally. He not only omits the Muses here; he is very sparing with classical allusion throughout.

Book I mentions the Cyclops, Circe, Thyestes, Medusa, the Centaurs, Vulcan, Atalanta, the dragon's teeth, and Hercules; Book II, a faun, the easy descent to Hades, the god of love, Pasithea, Narcissus, the Laestrigonians and Anthropophagi, the goddess Fame, Arion, and the Sibyl. Hector's arms are brought in as a piece of medieval derivation from Troy. Classical similes are inserted here and there, as if conscientiously: the meeting of two winds, fire in grain, a boar or bear at bay, two bulls or two lions. Nor does Boiardo strive for other ornament. His heightening is rather the sheer extravagance of epic brag.

Their blows were heard nearly a mile in the wood (I. iii. 59).

They came with such a battle-cry as made earth tremble, and sky and sea (I. iv. 51).

The moat brimmed with the blood of the slain (I. xi. 32).

Fire came to his heart and his face, and flamed from his helmet. He ground his teeth. His knees so clamped Brigliadoro that the mighty steed sank in the path (I. xv. 19).

The grinding of his teeth could be heard more than a bowshot (I. xv. 33).

Otherwise his words are usually as simple as Malory's. So far, classicism has made no headway in Renaissance verse narrative.

Boiardo's sentences, as Malory's, are typically aggregative, sometimes even crude. Instead of tightening a sentence or a stanza, he remains frankly diffuse. Fluent, sometimes slack, he runs on as if orally. His verse is pleasantly varied. Though he hardly ever lets a line end with a down-beat, he freely begins either up or down, or shifts to a dactyl. A stanza rarely runs over; but it is often linked with the next by refrain, as in popular poetry. Here and there the closing line of his octave sounds like an experiment in the direction followed later by Spenser. Inferior in stanza control to Boccaccio and to Ariosto, diffuse, somewhat careless, he is always agreeably and sometimes charmingly fluent.

Yet description, which became a regular Renaissance cue for dilation, Boiardo handles economically. Even where he is conventional he does not dilate; and usually he is both distinct and concise.

That spring was all adorned with white and polished alabaster, and so richly with gold that it shone in the flowery mead (I. iii. 33).

A fair rich palace made of marble polished so smooth as to mirror the whole garden (I. viii. 2).

Secret gardens of fresh verdure are above on the roofs and hidden on the ground. Gems and gold pattern all these noble and joyous places. Clear springs unstintingly fresh are surrounded by shady thickets. Above all, the place has an odor to give oppressed hearts their joy again (I. viii. 5).

His stories pictured on walls (*depintura istoriata*) whether fresco or mosaic, have a literary source. They are from the Troy stories pictured on the walls of Dido's palace in *Aeneid* II. Boiardo's briefer rendering may have been suggested by the "epigrams" of the Greek *Anthology,* or by survivals in southern Italy of such pictures with verse inscriptions. Certainly his palaces and gardens often recall the Norman-Arab art of Sicily. For it is art that he pauses to note oftener than scenery. In all this his classicism is both discreet and artistic. He does not borrow; he adapts.

The larger scene, the field of the traditional struggle of East with West, receives more definite geography. The haze over medieval Ermonie had been often pierced by merchant voyagers. Though there are still the Isole Felice or Lontane, we read now of Aragon and Barcelona, Granada, Toledo, Seville, Valencia, and Gibraltar; of Agrigentum and Mongibello as well as of Sicily at large; of Cyprus, Crete, and Rhodes; of Aigues Mortes, Bordeaux, Gascony, Languedoc, Perpignan, and Roussillon; of Damascus, Niniveh, Trebizond, and Tripoli.

The traditional chivalric equality of Saracen knights with Christian, as in Malory, is emphasized.

King Charles the Great with genial face had seated himself among his paladins at the round table. Before him were also Saracens, who would not use chair nor bench, but lay like mastiffs on their rugs, scorning the usage of the Franks (I. i. 12–13).

The paynim king Balugante, divining Rinaldo's irritation at some of his fellow Christians, sends him a courteous and discerning message. Saracen knights are armed, titled, respected as are Christian, and mingle with them freely. Their bravery is not merely admitted; Rodomonte is a legendary demon of force, and Ruggiero in his pagan days is a pattern of both force and courtesy.

The traditional echoes of folklore are repeated. Feraguto's strength revives when he touches earth. A child stolen in infancy is recognized. Herbs are gathered under a new moon. Ruggiero, as Percival, is brought up beyond sight of arms. There are waters of forgetfulness, a loathly lady waiting to be restored by a kiss, a magic steed, a white hart, a monster adversary transformed, and a retreat under water.

Grotesque interludes, barely touched by Malory, found occasionally elsewhere, and quite regular in Italian popular versions, are not only admitted by Boiardo; they are dwelt upon with evident relish. Thus Rinaldo fights with a giant.

Of no avail the furious assault; of no avail the baron's nimble skill. He could not reach so high. Suddenly Rinaldo dismounted and with one bound leapt upon the giant's croup when he was not looking. He knocked his helm and his steel cap to pieces and, redoubling his strokes as if he were hammering iron at the furnace, he split the great head in two. Fell the giant with a rush that made the earth shake (I. iv. 64–65).

Orlando leapt even higher, so that again and again he met his giant face to face—in the air. Angelica threw into a monster's mouth a cake that stuck his teeth together, so that Rinaldo might safely, though with enormous effort, strangle him. Rodomonte bare-headed at sea hears his hair rattle with ice. Astolfo is beguiled to board a whale, and Rinaldo follows, both on horseback.

On Bayard he plunged into the sea after the great fish in desperation. That whale went slowly, slowly; for it is very large and by nature grave (II. xiii. 65).

Marfisa, the woman knight, had her horse stolen and pursued the thief long in vain. The conception is grotesque; the execution, pure farce.

A fortnight had she followed him, nor was fed meantime on aught but leaves. The false thief, who was most astute, sped his flight with quite different food. For he was so quick and so bold that every tavern he saw he would enter and fall to eating, and then flee without paying his shot. And although the taverners and their waiters were after him with their pitchers and jugs in their hands, off he was, wiping his mouth and grinning (II. xv. 68–69).

Love, announced in the title *Orlando innamorato* and frequently asserted, has little more scope in Boiardo than in Malory. Whether the title expresses an original intention abandoned, or an appeal to court ladies, or merely a certain period in the hero's life, Boiardo's interest was elsewhere.

Long time Morgan, Alcina, and their magic wiles have kept me waiting; nor have I shown you a good sword-stroke (II. xiv. 1).

The good sword-stroke is what he gives with both hands, even as Malory.

Since the main interest is single combat, and all the fighters, even the Saracens, are memorable, there is a long roll of persons. Of the hundred mentioned in the first five cantos about a third never reappear; few are characterized consecutively; none is consecutively in action for any considerable period. The long poem is frankly a series, not a sequence. Boiardo's usual method is to carry one of his stories to a crisis, leave it to pick up another, and so on.

Let us now return to Astolfo, who remained, you know, alone at the fountain (I. ii. 17).[4]

[4] So I. iii. 31, 51; v. 13, 56; vi. 54; ix. 36; xi. 46; and throughout the poem.

As the Carolingian recitals on the piazza, or behind the marionettes, the *Orlando innamorato* may be entered at almost any point. What is there heard or read is interesting mainly for itself, very little as arising from previous action and characterization or as preparing for what follows. To say, then, that it fuses the two cycles is quite misleading. Boiardo brings in an Arthurian name, Tristan or Lancelot, as simply as he adds another Carolingian. He puts Merlin's well in the forest of Ardenne. He interpolates Morgan le Fay among the Orlando stories. But fusion, whether of these Arthurians or of his own Carolingians, is not in all his thoughts. He is engaged not in composing the Carolingian story, but in rehearsing the Carolingian stories.

Boiardo's *Orlando,* then, is a collection of heroes fighting in the struggle between East and West. Within that frame, as within the frame of Arthur's Round Table, tradition had collected many stories. Boiardo finds room for them, and even for others quite unrelated. Those of the greatest knights, Orlando, Rinaldo, Oliver, and their ladies and friends, the obligatory stories, he can tell by installments because they are familiar and have been already connected. The others he inserts here and there for variety. Not only does he accept the medieval cyclical aggregation, he ignores the later medieval achievement of narrative sequence in smaller scope through characterization.

A certain Tisbina, who has nothing to do with Charlemagne, is in much the same dilemma as Chaucer's Dorigen in the Franklin's Tale; and her Iroldo's response is much the same as that of Dorigen's Arveragus. Chaucer's solution is convincing, in spite of impossible marvels, because it is motivated by Dorigen's character. Boiardo's solution is inferior because it is quite extraneous and casual. His Tisbina is not characterized sufficiently to motivate the story toward any convincing issue.

Much less is Boiardo concerned to motivate his whole story. His Orlando in love is even removed for long stretches from the great struggle; and Boiardo interrupts both the love and the struggle to tell of Tisbina and Iroldo or insert a *fabliau*.[5] True, his poem remained unfinished; but evidently he had no idea of making it a coherent whole. His Latin and Greek did not suggest to him the shaping of verse narrative. Discernible in his style, though never intrusive, they do not move his composition; for composition was not his concern. Ignoring alike the medieval progress and Pulci's narrative cleverness with his own material, he was content with abundant activity, variety, and fluency.

But in another use of the classics he forecast the Renaissance habit of encomium. Ruggiero, legendary ancestor of his Ferrara patrons, brought up in paganism and remote from deeds of arms, is sought by Agramante for his great expedition against the Christian West. Ruggiero's aged tutor warns Agramante against the ultimate consequences of taking the marvelous youth into France. Charlemagne, he says, may be defeated, and our pride and courage enhanced;

[5] I. xxii is *fabliau;* and so, in various degrees, the stories inserted at I. vi. 22, xiii. 29, xxix. 3; II. i. 22, xiii. 9, xxvi. 22; III. ii. 47.

. . . but afterward the youth will become Christian, and—ah! traitress house of Maganza, which heaven should not tolerate on earth—in the end Ruggiero shall have through thee his death.

Would that were the final grief! But his descendants shall remain Christian, and come to honor as great as any the world knows today. They shall keep all, all generosity, all courtesy, sweet love and joyous state in a house the flower of the world.

I see Hugo Alberto di Sansogna descend to the Paduan plain, expert in arms, in intellect, in all the ways of glory, generous, noble, and above all humane. Hear, ye Italians: I warrant you. He who comes with that standard in hand brings with him all your redemption. Through him shall Italy be filled with prowess.

I see Azzo I and Aldobrandino III, nor know which to call the greater; for the one has killed the traitor Anzolino; the other has broken the Emperor Henry. Behold another Rinaldo paladin. I say no more of him than Lord of Vicenza, of Treviso, of Verona, who strikes the crown from Frederick.

Nature shows forth her treasure. Lo! the marquis who lacks no point of honor. Blest the age, and happy they who shall live in a world so free! In his time the golden lilies shall be joined to that white eagle whose home is in heaven; and his domain shall be the flower of Italy from the one fair seacoast to the other.

And if the other son of Amphitryon, who there appears in habit of a duke, has as much mind to seize dominion as he has to follow good and flee evil, all the birds—not to say the men who act in this great play—would flock to obey him. But why should I gaze further into the future? Thou destroyest Africa, King Agramante (II. xxi. 54–59).

With reminiscence, perhaps, of Dante, this is obviously patterned on Vergil. The historical vision of the house

of Este has its model in the vision of the Augustans.
Encomium with Boiardo is neither so frequent nor so
fulsome as it was to become with Ariosto and with
Spenser. Was that, perhaps, one reason for his double
eclipse? He was first superseded by Ariosto and then
rewritten by Berni.

7. ARIOSTO

The brilliant *Orlando furioso* (1516) of Ludovico
Ariosto (1474–1533) is one of the most typical verse
narratives of the Renaissance, as it was the most popular.
More accomplished than Boiardo in diction, verse, and
composition, and more responsive to the Renaissance,
Ariosto still follows the same serial plan. The two poets
differ more in degree than in kind. Both were trained in
the classics; both began by writing Latin; both offer
romance as inspiring contrast with actuality.

O great hearts of those ancient knights! They were rivals;
they differed in religion; they still felt the rude and wicked
strokes aching throughout their bodies; and yet through dark
woods and crooked paths they went together without distrust
(i. 22).

[War has been debased through the diabolical invention of
artillery (xi. 22–25)]. How foundest thou ever place in
human hearts, O invention criminal and ugly! Through thee
military glory has been destroyed, through thee the craft of
arms dishonored, through thee valor and prowess so dimin-
ished that oft the knave seems better than the good soldier.

And though Rinaldo was not very rich in cities or treasure,
he was so affable and genial and so prompt to share with
them whatever he had that not one of his meinie was drawn

away by offer of more gold. A man of Montauban never forsakes it unless great need constrains him elsewhere (xxxi. 57).

O famished, deformed, fierce Harpies, who in blinded and
misguided Italy, perhaps as punishment of ancient sins, bring
to every table divine judgment! Innocent children and faithful mothers drop with hunger while they see one feast of
these foul monsters devour what might have kept them
alive. . . [Italy cries] Is there no one of you . . to free your
tables from the filth and the claws . . as the paladin freed that
of the Ethiop king? (xxxvi. 1–3).

Encomium with Ariosto becomes pervasive. Animated
of course by the personal ends of a court poet, it serves
also the literary end of magnificence, the first aspect in
which the Renaissance viewed epic.

Who will give me the voice and the words fit for a subject so
noble? Who will lend me wings strong enough to attain my
lofty conception? Far greater than its customery heat must
be the poetic furor in my breast. For this part I owe my lord,
since it sings of the noble line from which he sprang.
    Among the illustrious lords issued from heaven to govern
the earth, never seest thou, O Phoebus who surveyest the
wide earth, a race more glorious in peace or in war, nor any
whose nobility has been kept longer, and shall be kept, if
that prophetic light which inspires me errs not, so long as
the heavens revolve about the pole (iii. 1–2).

The Vergilian vision of Augustan Rome is heard again
in Merlin's prophecy. Epic rolls of honor muster the
English warriors, the women of Este, even the painters.
Besides these are many incidental references, especially
at canto openings.

Of courtesy, of nobility, examples among the ancient warriors were many, and few are there among the moderns. But of impious ways enough was seen and heard in that war, Hippolito, whose captured standards thou hast used to adorn our temples, as thou broughtest to thy ancestral shores their captive galleys laden with prey (xxxvi. 2).

The mission of the poet to confer fame, proclaimed by Ariosto and repeated by Ronsard, is also seen in bitter contrast. The speaker is St John the Evangelist.

So worthy men are snatched from oblivion worse than death by poets. O intelligent and wise princes who follow the example of Augustus in making writers your friends, and thus need not fear the waves of Lethe. Poets, as singing swans, are rare, poets not unworthy of the name; for heaven prevents too great abundance of famous ones by the great fault of stingy lords, who by oppressing excellence and exalting vice banish the noble arts. We may suppose that God has deprived these ignorant men of their wits and darkens their light of reason in making them shy of poetry, that death may quite consume them. For wicked as their ways might be, if only they knew how to win the friendship of Apollo they might rise from their graves in sweeter odor than nard or myrrh.

Aeneas was not so pious, nor Achilles so mighty, as their fame, nor Hector so brave. There have been thousands and thousands who might with truth have been put before them; but the palaces or great villas bestowed by their descendants have given them sublime honors without end at the honored hands of writers. Augustus was neither so holy nor so benign as sounds the trumpet of Vergil; but his having good taste in poetry brings him pardon for his unjust proscription. Not would he who had against him earth and hell have the less fame, perhaps, if he knew how to keep the writers his friends.

Homer made Agamemnon victorious, the Trojans cowardly and dull, and Penelope constant to her husband through the thousand persecutions of the suitors. If you wish to uncover the truth, convert the story to its contrary; that the Greeks were routed, Troy the victor, and Penelope a harlot. On the other hand hear how fame leaves Dido, whose heart was so chaste, to be reputed a baggage, only because Vergil was not her friend. Wonder not that I am oppressed thereat, and that I speak of it at such length. I love writers and pay them what I owe; for in your world I too was a writer (xxxv. 22–28).

This strange parenthesis of satire, dubious in its humor, shocking in its irreverence, sounds today like encomium reduced to advertisement. It sounds also like the bitter retort of realism to that fiction of the courtier which was to have literary vogue through Castiglione. Bitter and foul the actual wars of Italy in contrast to old chivalry; but bitter also the trade of those who sing them.

Though often oratorical, Ariosto rarely seeks his magnificence by elaboration of style. He has too much taste, too much concern for popular appeal. He even admits the appeal of the traditional epic brag. Rodomonte alone sacks a city; Grifone throws a knight over the wall; great rocks are hurled from ships; and—triumph of rodomontade—the fragments of a combat fly up to the sphere of fire and come down lighted.

There are a few reminiscences of the *Aeneid,* fewer of Horace, fewest of Dante and Petrarch. Classical allusion has become a common decoration. Aurora is already obligatory for dawn. Occasionally a classical periphrasis ("Hardly had the Licaonian seed turned her plow through the furrows of heaven" xx. 82) is obscure; or there is incongruity in combining Avernus and the Sibyl with Merlin's grotto, or the Fates with Death, Nature, and St John. But allusion is neither paraded nor often intruded. Classical similes, much more frequent than with Boiardo, are evidently sought for decoration. They are one of the signs that Ariosto's time thought of epic in terms of style. But they are used also for vividness; and they range widely. Besides those drawn conventionally from beasts of prey or from storm, there are many quite sharply individual: wood steaming in a fire, grass ebbing and flowing in the wind, a pile-driver, and a mine cave-in. Ariosto's decoration is rarely a hindrance, rarely even elaborate. He is easy to read. The bearing of a passage here and there may be dubious because of looseness in the narrative, but never its meaning. He has reconciled dignity with popularity. Instead of posing as literary, he makes his readers feel literary themselves. He puts them at ease in fine company.

In sentence and stanza movement Ariosto has made his poem easy to read by diffuse and various fluency. Writing for entertainment, he uses balance or other word-play only as occasional means of variety. He is neither sententious nor pretentious. His metrical skill, remarkable in range and control, is not put forward for exhibition; it is an accompaniment so flexible to mood as constantly to enhance the connotation. Rarely lengthening the final line of the stanza often using refrain to link stanzas, and sometimes within stanzas, he is most characteristic in making the *ottava rima* run on not only from line to line, but from stanza to stanza. This fluent ease is by no means impromptu spontaneity. It is the work of ten years. His diffuseness, then, is not carelessness; it is adjustment alike to the immediate audience of the court and to the increasing readers of the press.

Especially significant, therefore, is his handling of description. His landscape is often both brief and conventional.

Winsome thickets of pleasant laurel, of palms and gayest myrtle, of cedar, of orange with fruit and flowers woven in forms most various and all beautiful, make a refuge from the fervid heat of summer days with their thick parasols; and among these branches in safe flight nightingales go singing.

Among the purpled roses and the white lilies, which the warm air keeps ever fresh, rabbits and hares are seen at peace, and deer, heads high and proud, without fear that any one may kill or take them, feed or chew their cud at rest. Swift and nimble leap the harts and goats that abound in those country places (vi. 21–2).

But he has a way of animating convention with a sharp word of his own.

When the trembling brooks (*trepidi ruscelli*) began to loosen the cold ice in their warm waves (xii. 72).

Architecture and decoration often remain generalized, or offer few details. Ampler is pageantry.

With triumphal pomp and great festivity they return together into the city, which is green with branches and garlands. All the streets are hung with tapestries. A shower of herbs and flowers spreads from above and falls upon and around the victors, cast in handfuls from loggias and fair windows by ladies and damsels.

In various places where they turn a corner they find improvised arches and trophies displaying pictures of the ruins and fires of Biserta and other worthy deeds; elsewhere, balconies with divers games and spectacles and mimes and plays; and at every corner is inscribed the true title: To the Liberators of the Empire.

With sound of shrill trumpets and mellow clarinets, with harmony of every instrument, mid laughter and applause, joy and favor of the people, who could hardly come close enough, the great Emperor dismounted at the palace, where several days that company stayed to enjoy itself with tournaments, *personnages* and farces, dances and banquets (xliv. 32–34).

This is a preciously distinct picture of actual Renaissance pageantry. More vividly detailed is the funeral of Brandimarte. Even these, however, are not dilated. They are appropriate to their narrative function. The long descriptive summary of Astolfo's journey through the Valley of the Moon is an interlude of satire; and Orlando's battle with the monster Orc is pure grotesque. He rows into the Orc's mouth, casts anchor there, and, when the monster plunges, tows him ashore. Moreover, both these are narrated; neither is a descriptive pause.

Ariosto does pause, however, to dilate description of the beauty of women. Seven stanzas enumerate the charms of the enchantress Alcina (vii. 10–16).

The fair palace excelled not so much in surpassing the richness of every other as in having the most delightful folk in the world and the noblest. Little did one differ from another in flowered age and in beauty; only Alcina was most beautiful of all, as the sun is more beautiful than any star.

In person she was as well formed as the industry of painters can imagine: her blond hair long and tressed; gold is not more splendid and lustrous. Rose mingled with hawthorn white spread over her delicate cheek. Of polished ivory was her joyous forehead, and of just proportion.

Beneath two black and fine-spun brows are two black eyes, as two clear suns, sympathetic in gaze, frugal in movement, about which Love seems to sport and fly, and from which he empties his quiver and visibly steals hearts. Thence descends a nose in which Envy herself could find no fault.

Beneath this, as between two valleys, the mouth besprent with native cinnabar, wherein are two rows of choice pearls, enclosed or opened by fair, sweet lips, whence issues speech of courtesy fit to soften even a base heart, and whence rises the winsome laughter that brings paradise to its place on earth [and so on for three more stanzas].

This is the conventional description called by the Middle Age *blason*. It is used again for Olimpia bound to the rock, where the situation itself is conventional. A bit of very old folklore, and coming down also through classical mythology as Perseus and Andromeda, it was a commonplace for dilation.

But what Ariosto dilates oftenest is emotion. His characteristic pauses are lyric. Thus he interpolates the medieval *compleint d'amour* not only again and again, but for long exhalations. Bradamante alone utters a whole series of these laments. The second begins as follows:

Then shall it be true (said she) that I must seek him who flees me and hides? Then must I prize him who scorns me? Must I implore him who never answers me? Shall I endure to hold at heart him who hates me, who thinks his qualities so rare that an immortal goddess must descend from heaven to kindle his heart with love?

In his pride he knows that I love him, that I adore him;

nor will he of me for lover nor for slave. In his cruelty he knows that I yearn and die for him; and he waits till after death to give me help. And lest I tell him of my martyrdom, fit to move even his stubborn will, he hides himself from me, as the asp who to keep her venom refuses to hear the charm.

Ah! Love, stay him who hastes so free beyond my slow running, or restore me to the state whence thou hast taken me, when I was subject neither to thee nor to any other. Alas! how deceitful and foolish is my hope that ever prayers should move thee to pity! For thou delightest to draw streams of tears from our eyes; nay, thereon thou feedest and livest (xxxii. 18–20).

Substantially the same is the famous madness of Orlando. Though Ariosto cleverly gives it narrative enough to relieve its prolongation through twenty-five stanzas, it is a dilated lyric interlude.

The art that dilates these lyrics is rhetoric. Thus they answer not only the learning, but the taste of the Renaissance. With Alcina's charms and Olimpia's, they were the favorite passages of the Pléiade. Ronsard, using them often, was especially fond of Orlando's madness. Beyond the Pléiade, they open a long vista toward Italian opera. To look the other way, back to the Middle Age, is to meet the sharp contradiction of Dante. Paolo and Francesca, or Ugolino, is the poetic antithesis to Bradamante and Orlando.

Such dilated interludes would interrupt any progress of the whole story; and they are not the only interpolations. Traditionally the cyclical romances might pause to add incidental stories, usually told by errant damsels seeking help. Ariosto inserts these freely, and quite as

freely others having even less relevance. The story of
Ginevra, Ariodante, and Polinesso (Canto V), for instance, though it falls among Rinaldo's adventures, has
its own intrigue and motivation. Equally separable, the
fabliau of Fiammetta is told for sex, and prolonged by
appended dialogue and comment. "Ladies," it begins,
"and you who hold ladies in esteem, for heaven's sake
give no ear to this story. . . Omit this canto; for my story
needs it not and will be no less clear without it." Evidently Ariosto has not planned his cantos as chapters.

A mere glance through the summaries prefixed to each
canto will show that the many interruptions are not breaks
in the sequence of the whole. There is no such sequence.
The poem is a collection of parallel stories taken up in
turn, and only thus combined, not integrated in a single
scheme. Accepting Boiardo's method, he uses the same
frank transitions.

But to another time I will defer the story of what ensued
from this. I must return to the good King Charles, against
whom Rodomonte was coming in haste and whose folk he
was killing (xviii. 8).

He even turns them to humor.

I am reminded that I ought to tell you (I promised to, and
then I forgot) of a suspicion that the fair lady of the griev-
ing Ruggiero had concerning the other lady less pleasing and
more wicked and of sharper and more venomous tooth, so
that through what she heard from Ricciardetto it devoured
the heart in her breast.

I should have told you, and I began something else because
Rinaldo intervened; and then Guidone gave me enough to do,
so that he held me off a bit on the way. From one thing to

another I became so involved that I hardly remembered Bradamante. I remember her now, and I am going to go on with her story before I tell of Rinaldo and Gradasso.

Before I speak of her, need is that I speak a bit of Agramante (xxxii. 1–3).

Such narrative art as Ariosto exhibits is in detail, not in the onwardness of the whole story. The close is both interrupted and delayed.

Canto XXXVI, which finally brings Ruggiero and Bradamante together, ends without their actual reunion. There is no meeting, no dialogue. Canto XXXVIII takes Ruggiero from her, to support his honor; "and that, ladies, is strange." Canto XLIV still postpones, as lesser issues have been postponed, *the* issue, their marriage. Canto XLVI ends characteristically on description of the wedding and encomium of Ariosto's patron Ippolito; but that the poem may conclude as the *Aeneid* with the defeat of Turnus, it gives Ruggiero one more victory. Boccaccio's art of the long narrative poem, to say nothing of Chaucer's, is ignored.

This is not careless; it is intentional. Some of the delay at the close was added in the final revision of 1532. Ariosto designed not sequence, but abundance and variety. His opening *Arma virumque cano* is: "I sing the ladies, the loves, the courtesies, the bold emprise of the time when the Moors crossed the sea from Africa and did such harm in France. . . Of Orlando too will I tell, how for love he went mad." These loves, traditional in still subscribing to *amour courtois,* are more various than Boiardo's. But though much of the appeal is by amorous descant, the staple of this Carolingian romance is still single combat. As for Orlando's love madness, announced in the title and in the opening lines, it is not reached till Canto XXIII; and once his fury is spent, he disappears once more for some six cantos. He is hardly even a leading character. The principal role, for encomium of the house of Este, belongs to Ruggiero. Stories of the other paladins are often brought into connection, sometimes skillfully, sometimes ingeniously, rarely to the extent of making a situation, never in such an onward scheme as Chaucer's *Troilus and Criseyde.* For that demands what Ariosto never sought, consistent motivation by progressive characterization from scene to scene. Such characterization as Ariosto offers remains separate. Zerbino has more space than is warranted by any distinct function. Oliver, coming in casually, is less a person than a great traditional name. Astolfo's miraculous journey, with its interesting geographical list has so little visible function that it might as well have been made somewhere else, or by some one else. Leone, one of the most distinct characterizations, comes in only toward the end. Even Ruggiero meets Bradamante when he least expects or deserves her.

Ariosto is a typical example of the popular poet gauging and answering his public. His elegant ease is flattering. His decoration is distinct. His diffuseness relieves us of all coöperative thinking. A scene is dilated through every phase of its emotion, and then discharged as finished in and for itself. The next will be pleasantly different, or, if unpleasantly, may be skipped. The dilation, the variety, that Vergil turned his back upon, and

after him Tasso, Ariosto frankly sought. He has no care
for poetic sequence beyond neat transitions, no poetic
austerity of sustained single purpose. Renaissance poets,
for all the cult of classicism, often revived the ancient
world in Alexandrian decadence, saw in Vergil only his
high style, conceived poetic as rhetoric, and ran after the
"Greek Romances." Ariosto was one of these Alexan-
drians.

8. TASSO AND SPENSER

The contrast between Tasso and Spenser is heightened
by the fact that they were closely contemporary. Spenser's
birth was eight years after Tasso's; his death, but three
years. Tasso began his *Gerusalemme liberata* in his twen-
ties, published it at thirty-one, kept it on his mind
throughout his working life, and finally rewrote it.
Spenser published three books of his *Faerie Queene* at
thirty-eight, three more at forty-three, and left it unfinished. Tasso's is the shortest of the Renaissance verse
romances; Spenser's was to be the longest. Tasso turned
away from Ariosto toward Vergil; Spenser moved even
farther than Ariosto from epic sequence. Allegory, hardly
more than a figure of speech with Tasso, is announced
by Spenser as his plan. Religion having more place in
these two romances than in any of the others, Tasso's is
conceived as uniting western Europe, Spenser's as nationalistic. Tasso's poem is one of the greater European books,
and has been widely read in England; Spenser's great
reputation has been very slow to cross the Channel. The
latter years of the sixteenth century, then, carried on verse
romance in two distinct directions: the classical direction

from Aristotelian theory and Vergilian practice toward narrative singleness and sequence; the allegorizing of the medieval cycles toward a series of counsels for individual and social conduct.

(a) *Tasso*

Tasso's is the only one of the Renaissance romances of chivalry whose title is its subject. Malory's subject is far more than the death of Arthur, Pulci's than Morgante. Boiardo's subject is not Orlando in love, nor Ariosto's Orlando mad for love. Spenser's title merely makes his encomium part of his allegory. But Tasso's *Jerusalem Delivered* exactly sums up his scope and his theme. The Carolingian tradition, still furnishing the scene and the persons, no longer furnishes the pattern. The persons are fewer; and they are recreated to function in a continuous story. Thus Soliman and Peter the Hermit have definite roles; and Godfrey becomes the protagonist. The time is idealized to assemble the heroic past about the medieval enterprise of deliverance, to bring into one sequence the *chansons de geste,* the Carolingian cycle of romance, and several crusades. The struggle of the West with the East, no longer background or setting, is brought forward. It appears much less as the exploits of individuals, much more as an enterprise in common. Further it is an enterprise of religion, to rescue the holy places from unbelievers, to restore them to Christendom as a shrine of pilgrimage. It is animated by *pietas,* the Vergilian motive Christianized, the sense of mission. The individual warriors, no longer adventurers, are soldiers of the Cross. Though the actual crusades were medieval, they were still in men's minds as unfinished. Boiardo laments the postponement of a recent proposal to revive them. Tasso writes not to further this, or any other present movement, but to present crusade as historic. He focuses all crusades in one historic action. His narrative of Godfrey and the paladins is controlled by the idea of crusade as deliverance.

Such singleness of purpose naturally reduces encomium. The expected rolls of honor celebrating the house of Este, are fewer and more detached.[6] Reduced also, with one important exception, are lyric interludes. Turning conventional themes to beauty, Tasso pauses less often to dilate emotion with Ariosto than to interpose reflection or the escape of pastoral.

[In the garden of Armida] See how the rose pricks modest and virgin from the green. Half-open yet, half-closed, the less she shows herself the fairer she. Lo! bold already, she reveals her breast naked; lo! again it droops and is not seen. It is not seen which had been desired by a thousand maids and a thousand lovers.

> So passes, at the passing of a day,
> Of mortal life the flower and the green.
> April cannot be halted nor return
> To flower again, to green a second spring.
> Gather we roses handsome as the morn
> Of this our day, which soon will lose its calm,
> Roses of love. Ah! let us love betimes,
> When loving we may still be loved again (xvi. 14–15).[7]

Scenery, handled with the usual Italian restraint, is often woven expertly into the narrative. We are made to

---

[6] E. Donadone, *Torquato Tasso* (Venice, 1928).
[7] The stanzas are adapted by Spenser, FQ, Book II. xii. 74–75.

feel Jerusalem before it is described; and the grave and restrained description of the great Mass is inseparable from the action. Tasso's subordination of literary means to literary function dominates his style. The frequency of his classical similes is apparent only on review; it does not challenge attention, much less interrupt. His classical allusions are not extraneous decoration, much less parade. His word-play is used oftenest to mark the close of a stanza. His verse is harmonized. These are various aspects of artistic conscience. Tasso never plays the virtuoso; he is too great an artist.

The onwardness of the whole story, which is most distinctive in this achievement, could hardly be carried out in Tasso's time with entire consistency. Though there is none of the former easy shifting from tale to tale, though tactics and strategy are made to control and subordinate the traditional single combats, there are a few interpolated tales: Sofronia and Olindo in Canto II; Sven, isolated and picturesque in Canto VIII; Clorinda's origin in Canto XII. Canto X is less a stage than a pause to tell what was said and thought on one side and on the other. The enchantment of the wood in Canto XIII is a parenthesis in the siege. The most serious deviation is for Rinaldo and Armida. Armida has too much stage—as Dido has in the *Aeneid,* yes, but with less warrant. While the siege waits, Cantos XIV and XV detail the infatuation of Rinaldo and linger over the journey for his recall. Nothing of this counts for the sequence of the poem but his defection at a critical point and his return. The rest is dilated for its own picturesqueness and passion. But the flaw is conspicuous only because Tasso's sequence is beyond any previous attempt. The Rinaldo episode could be added without disturbance, here or there, in Boiardo's poem, Ariosto's, or Spenser's. Tasso has taught us to expect more.

To a degree hitherto unattained in the romances, and rarely even attempted, his persons are characterized for their function. Even Armida thus functions early (Canto V) in the whole scheme as disintegrating. She is more than a type of enchantress, more than a personification of lust. Though toward the end her despair at losing Rinaldo may be too oratorical and too much like Dido's, her revenge breaks down for love. In other cases, too, magic and demons are more acceptable because the visible human motives and action reduce them almost to figures of speech. For instance, the magic borrowed from the *Aeneid* in Canto X is merely a device for having Soliman present, acting in his own fate. Personifications are rare; and even the stock hermit has more distinct function. Godfrey is much more than Arthur or Charlemagne. His largeness of view is at once intelligence and faith. A cardinal example of Tasso's art is the creative use of the archangel St Michael. He comes as light and allies the heavenly host to the earthly. *Jerusalem Delivered* is not only the integration of the traditional hero stories; it is also the realization of the Renaissance dream of epic.

(*b*) *Spenser*

Spenser's most obvious peculiarity of style is archaism. Some of the *arts poétiques* repeat perfunctorily the rhetorical advice to revive old words; but none of the other romancers follows it with conviction. Though archaism is historically one of the habits of sophistic oratory, with Spenser it was animated rather by the desire to revive the English poetic tradition. Failing in this through ignorance of language, he but made his diction more difficult.

The style of the *Faerie Queene* is of its time in decorative classical similes. In classical allusions Spenser leans more heavily on legend and mythology. Sometimes he inserts lore gratuitously. Throughout he throws together classical and medieval, Christian, and pagan.[8] Occasionally mythology is made a vehicle for contemporary politics and religion. Usually decorative, his mythology is generally incidental, not functional. Thus his angels, too, are disappointing beside Tasso's.

Following thus generally the Renaissance habit of learned elegance, Spenser shows his own hand in concreteness. He is less often content with mere epithet. He specifies even the details of a kitchen; and he specifies habitually in abundant sensory images, even of ugliness.

> Therewith she spewd out of her filthie maw
> A floud of poyson horrible and blacke,
> Full of great lumps of flesh and gobbets raw,
> Which stunck so vildly that it forst him slacke
> His grasping hold, and from her turne him backe:
> Her vomit full of bookes and papers was,
> With loathly frogs and toades, which eyes did lacke,
> And creeping sought way in the weedy grass.
> Her filthie parbreake all the place defiled has (I. i. 20).

[8] Diocletian-giants-Brutus-Hogh-Gormet-Hercules, II. x. 7; Tristan-nymphs-Latona's son, VI. ii. 25.

Oftener picturesque, such vividness decorates even the traditional extravagance.

> Thus long they trac'd and traverst to and fro,
> And tryde all waies, how each mote entrance make
> Into the life of his malignant foe;
> They hew'd their helmes, and plates asunder brake,
> As they had potshares bene; for nought mote slake
> Their greedy vengeaunces but goary blood,
> That at the last like to a purple lake
> Of bloudy gore congeal'd about them stood,
> Which from their riven sides forth gushed like a flood
>   (VI. i. 37)

For Spenser's diction is habitually overloaded. The verse is surcharged with alliteration.

> O how great *s*orrow my *s*ad *s*oule as*s*aid (I. ii. 24).

> Sometimes her head she fondly would a*g*uize
> With *g*audy *g*irlonds or *f*resh *f*lowers dight
> About her necke, or *r*ings of *r*ushes plight (II. vi. 7).

> Day and night keeping *w*ary *w*atch and *w*ard
> For *f*eare least *F*orce or *F*raud should unaware
> Breake in (II. vii. 25).

> That her *b*road *b*eauties *b*eam great *b*rightness threw (II. vii. 45).

Spenser's metric, often obscured by fanciful spelling or uncertain pronunciation, is expertly varied. The Spenserian stanza, undoubtedly skillful, is nevertheless inferior to the Italian octave for narrative. It carries on with less ease. The sheer metrical task of the six completed books (3,732 stanzas, or 33,588 lines) was beyond Spenser's revision. Some rhymes remain forced by stilted transposition, or upon insignificant words, as in the last line of the first example above, and in:

And henceforth ever wish that like succeed it may (I. i. 27).
And each the other from to rise restraine (II. ii. 64).

Though he uses expertly the variation of throwing together two stresses, he has also left many lines clogged with more than can be uttered without scanting or even stumbling. Thus in the second canto of the first book:

And to him calls "Rise, rise! unhappy swaine" (l. 4).
He could not rest; but did his stout heart eat (l. 6).
Did search, sore grieved in her gentle brest (l. 8).
O too deare love, love bought with death too deare! (l. 31).

In both style and verse the *Faerie Queene* is the least facile of the chivalric romances.

For the composition of the whole, Spenser's scheme is not narrative. The most descriptive of all the romancers, he has made his total effect not merely abundant separable ecphrasis but pageantry. For holding the pageantry together he proposes in his preface moral allegory, "fashioning a gentleman or noble person in vertuous and gentle discipline." This end, Caxton's preface to Malory proclaims, is attained without allegory, by the romances themselves as stories. But now romance, having been first rewritten in Renaissance style, and then recomposed as Vergilian epic, is to be moralized. Further, the allegory is political. Artegall is Lord Grey de Wilton; Duessa and Radegund, Mary Queen of Scots; Archimago, the Pope. The poem is anti-Catholic with the Elizabethan political bias. Its attacks on abuses of the Church, no louder than those of *Piers Plowman,* are essentially different in that Elizabethan England has broken with the medieval vision of unity. Spenser speaks for the most self-sufficient of the rising nations, and makes its national mission his own. For the divine mission of the poet in Renaissance classical phrase means practically the claim of the poet to support by the court. The new nationalism but intensifies encomium. Spenser was a court poet in the same way as Ariosto, and to an even greater degree. He celebrates not only England, but the Queen and his immediate patrons. He prefixes a letter to Raleigh and seventeen poems to lords and ladies; and he interposes the usual references and allusions. None of the chivalric romances is more devoted to encomium than the *Faerie Queene.*

To weave all these strands into any large single sequence is probably beyond the capacity of allegory, and certainly beyond Spenser's achievement. The legendary history of Britain in Book II has little enough to do with the theme of constancy; the long pastoral in Book VI with the theme of courtesy. Even single books, then, do not always hold together. Within a single virtue we have at most a medieval series of *exempla.* Even if Spenser had lived to subsume all his virtues in Magnificence, the Renaissance *virtú,* he would have achieved only the summary of a series. The earlier critics of the *Faerie Queene* were embarrassed by their obligation to consider it as epic. Spenser's quoting of the Horatian *in mediis rebus* "A poet thrusteth into the middest" in his preface, and his beginning thus "A gentle knight was pricking on the plaine" are merely superficial. No long poem is farther removed from epic than the *Faerie Queene*. Dryden, in a digression of his *Essay on Satire* (1693), said more significantly: "There is no uniformity of design in Spenser."

Instead of being ruled out as merely Dryden's preoccupation with French seventeenth-century "regularity," this may well be pondered. Later criticism of the romantic period, indeed, was inclined to reply: "What of it? The *Faerie Queene* offers so much else that we are content to dispense with uniformity of design." But still later criticism has not been so sure; and, what is more important, many readers have balked. The poem does not carry through. Today those who have read the six books are inclined to boast. Doubtless the forming of a gentleman has less appeal as an idea than Tasso's common enterprise of deliverance. Certainly the poetic machinery of knight errantry allegorized as the triumphs of virtues over vices has less appeal than crusade. Motive and method are insufficient to integrate the *Faerie Queene* and carry it forward. Its very timeliness has faded into insularity. *Don Quixote,* full of seventeenth-century Spain, is significant to the whole western world; the *Faerie Queene* is sometimes significant only in terms of Tudor politics. But probably the main reason for the waning of the *Faerie Queene* is the insufficiency of the conception to animate a long poem and of the composition to carry it forward. Beside *Paradise Lost,* to say nothing of the *Divina Commedia,* it is seen to have "no uniformity of design" in the sense of lacking effective integration.

Chapter VI

DRAMA

REVIVAL of drama is not a Renaissance achievement. The Renaissance has no drama distinctively its own. Even the sixteenth century prolonged a period of transition. Elizabethan comedy found new ways only in its last decade; Elizabethan tragedy, French tragedy and tragicomedy, matured in the seventeenth century. Medieval sacred plays continued, and the moralities proved too feeble dramatically to survive. Court shows of various kinds and degrees did, indeed, experiment dramatically with mythology, pastoral, and even rustic realism; but quite generally they lingered in allegory and pageantry, and their dramatic successes did not widen dramaturgy till 1590. While it practiced popular drama in *mystère* and *miracle,* the Middle Age had repeated that definition of drama which made it not so much a distinct form of composition as a style. This conception persisted through the Renaissance, especially in tragedy. Tragedy was still the fall of a prince; and it was rather a dialogue in high style than a sequence of action on the stage. Renaissance tragedy was classicized, indeed, in style; but in composition it remained as immune to the example of the Greek tragedians as the poetics[1] to the theory of Aristotle. It still imitated Seneca and quoted the "Ars poetica" of Horace. Often it was not even intended for the stage.

[1] Chapter VII.

Comedy had better auspices and somewhat earlier development. Plautus and Terence, already familiar to the Middle Age, had the great advantage of being acted. Latin school plays, translations, imitations, kept before the Renaissance the pattern of Latin Comedy. Narrow and conventional, but definite and stirring, this had been found adaptable to the *fabliau* situations of medieval farce, and was still active. Indeed, it was the starting point of many a Renaissance dramatist. Until Greek tragedy finally became active in dramaturgy, the only classical model for play composition that went beyond Seneca was Latin Comedy.

1. SACRED PLAYS

The most widespread stage drama of the fifteenth century was medieval. *Mystère* and *miracle, sacre rappresentazioni,* continued, indeed, well into the sixteenth century. The *Annales d'Aquitaine* of Jean Bouchet is quite specific.

The King of France, by his letters patent issued the 18th day of January, 1533, commanded all the nobles of Poitou . . . to appear with such [troops and equipment] as they owed for his service in the following May; and the review (*monstres*) was before the Seneschal of Poitou in the city of Poitiers . . . On the 14th of July the mayor, échevins, and bourgeois of Poitiers also gave their review for the king's service in the aforesaid city. And on the morrow were made joyous and triumphal presentations (*monstres*) of the mysteries of the Incarnation, Nativity, Passion, Resurrection, and Ascension of our Savior Jesus Christ, and of the mission given by the Holy Spirit, which mysteries were played for a fortnight in the old market of the aforesaid city, in a theater built most triumphally around it (*en un théatre fait en rond, fort triomphant*). And the aforesaid play began on Sunday, the 19th day of the aforesaid month, and lasted continuously for the eleven days following, wherein were very good actors and richly costumed. . . . The Passion and Resurrection were played also three weeks afterward, or thereabouts, in the city of Saumur, where I saw excellent acting (page 473 of the edition of 1644).

This description applies in essentials to the English Corpus Christi cycles, which we have in fifteenth-century texts, and to the general European tradition. What was that tradition in terms of drama? Typically a saint's legend (*miracle*) is less available for a play than a Bible story. The external life of a saint represented as a series of trials may be unwieldy or monotonous. The great moments of the Magdalen, indeed, have as clear stage possibilities as the sacrifice of Isaac; but generically the *miracles* yielded less effective drama than the *mystères*. The distinction between the two soon ceased to be current in England; there the word *miracle* came to be applied to either. *Mystère,* applied as above to Incarnation, Nativity, Passion, and so forth, refers more properly to a series than to a single play. Was there drama, then, in a whole series of sacred plays?

Yes, abstractly in idea, as when we speak of the drama of the Terror in France. But the dramatic values of a whole period can be only suggested; they are rather pervasive than controlling. The suggestion was heightened for the medieval audience by familiarity with the habit of conceiving the Old Testament as a prefiguration of the New and by typical characterization. In sculpture, glass, or poetry the Baptist is not only the immediate fore-runner; he is the last of the prophets. The burning bush is not only a portent for Moses; it prefigures the Virgin kindled but intact. Piers Plowman, besides being a particular person in a poem, is typically the *bon laboureur;* and on the higher plane he is the Good Shepherd. The medieval audience, alive to such suggestions, more readily saw in a given play the larger drama behind the particular action, felt the communal emotion, and took the typical experience to itself.

The series as a whole, however, sacred history presented as a scheme of divine providence, offered no specific training to a playwright. Abraham's sacrifice of Isaac should suggest the great sacrifice; but that would not make it a play. The immediate task was the realization of the immediate dramatic values: Isaac's growing fear, Abraham's cumulative struggle. Though the series included items intractable to representation, it offered many situations worthy of the highest skill. These the medieval dramatists had abundant practice in handling as distinct plays. The unknown authors show real dramatic experience and sometimes clear dramatic achievement. The English evidence is especially convincing. The guild, of course, keeping the scrip of a given play along with the costumes and properties, was free to revise or even to supersede. Some of the devices, such as the comic struggle with Noah's wife, evidently arose from the actual performance. None the less certain plays stand out as dramatically composed: the admirable progress of the Brome *Abraham and Isaac,* the diction of both Mary and Joseph so purely answering the action of the York *Nativity,* the rapid, direct, free handling of the Towneley *Secunda Pastorum.* The sacred plays, then, constituted within limits an important dramatic tradition; and that tradition was still active in the sixteenth century.

2. TRAGEDY

The tragedies of Seneca are so oratorical as to suggest rather declamation than acting.[2] The great persons of Greek tragedy, Oedipus, Medea, or the house of Atreus, are revived not to interact toward their doom, but to make speeches. Nevertheless the vogue of pieces so inferior as drama, holding over from the Middle Age, had long and wide Renaissance authority. There is no clearer example alike of the preoccupation with oratory and of the habit of conceiving poetic as rhetoric. The printing of the great Greek plays, and even their translation, were slow in counteracting Seneca. Nor was Seneca altogether a hindrance. Encouraging the fustian or dullness of lesser men, he invited the magnificence of Marlowe. But he delayed the progress of dramaturgy by confirming the Renaissance neglect of composition for style.

"There is no one in France," says Turnebus in a note[3] to his friend's tragedies, "with any pretensions to the humanities but knows George Buchanan." The humanists, lest after all their eminence in Latin should not be ratified by posterity, prudently praised one another. Joseph Scaliger called Buchanan the first Latin poet of Europe

[2] For Seneca, see ARP.
[3] *Opera,* II, 2.

(*ommes post se relinquens in Latina poesi*), as Heinsius was to call Joseph Scaliger the greatest scholar and man of letters. The complacent certitudes have suffered so much from the irony of time that we should be careful to give the sixteenth-century humanists their due. The type of international scholar for whom Latin was the literary language persisted in Buchanan (1506–1582). Spending some thirty years in France, he may have been more familiar with French than with his northern vernacular; but all his writing was in Latin. Such a humanist might well sustain his rank in Latin poetry not only by lyric verse and didactic, but also by dramatic (*Georgii Buchanani Scoti . . . opera omnia,* ed. Ruddiman, Edinburgh, 1715; Vol. II, "Poemata," dated 1714), and is quite typical of Renaissance tragedy in Latin.

His Latin translation of the *Medea* of Euripides seems to have been presented by students at Bordeaux in 1543.[4] His *Jephthes,* printed at Paris in 1554, recalls the passage of the Red Sea classically.

> Quum, te jubente, pigra moles aequoris
> Posuit procellas, mobilis stupuit liquor
> Cursu coacto, et vitreus crystallino
> Muro pependit pontus hinc et hinc, viam
> Praebere jussus (p. 5).

Serial iteration is sharpened by antithesis.

> Ut trudit undas unda, fluctus fluctui
> Cedit sequenti, pellitur dies die;
> Sempee premuntur praeterite novis malis;
> Dolor dolori, luctui est luctus comes (p. 2).

[4] "Acta fuit Burdegalae Anno MDXLIII" in the colophon can hardly mean merely that the play was finished in that year.

The capable verse rises to metrical skill in the choruses. In *Baptistes* (1576) the first chorus points with epigram the Sapphic familiar to the Middle Age.

> Occulit falsus pudor impudentem,
> Impium celat pietatis umbra,
> Turbidi vultu simulant quieta,
>   Vera dolosi (p. 19).

Classicism is even certified by pagan phrase; but there is no classical dramatic composition. In all its declamation and debate *Jephthes* has little dramatic movement. The long speeches of *Baptistes* hardly achieve even characterization. If Buchanan had learned from Euripides what made *Medea* a play, he was not making one himself; he was casting Latin poetry in dialogue and dividing oratory into five acts. In this he is typical of humanistic Latin tragedy. Learned, allusive, competent in style, it is not drama.

Classical tragedy in the vernacular is sufficiently exemplified by Robert Garnier (1544–1590, *Œuvres*, ed. Lucien Pinvert, Paris, 1923, 2 vols.). Knowing Greek tragedy as well as Seneca, appreciative, capable in style, making some dramatic advance in his seven tragedies from 1568 to 1583, he yet stopped short of the Greek type of composition, the dramaturgy that reduces a story to its crisis in order to move the play by compelling sequence of action. For his tragedies, though some of them may have been presented, were poems written to be read.

The argument of *Porcie* (1568) closes thus:

"Here, then, is the summary of the history on which I have planned this tragedy. You will find it in Dio's 47th book, in

Appian's 4th and 5th, and in Plutarch's lives of Cicero, Brutus, and Antony. I have also interwoven the fiction of the death of the Nurse, to involve it further with gloom and sorrow and make the catastrophe more bloody."

Act I consists of (1) a monologue by the Fury Mégère, a fine piece to say, and (2) a chorus of six rhymed stanzas. It is rather a prelude than an act.

In Act II Portia's monologue is followed by a chorus imitating Horace's second Epode, and the Nurse's monologue by their dialogue and another Horatian chorus. There is no action. The dialogue gives a hint of characterization when Portia in her doubt and fear regrets the death of Caesar.

Act III. Upon a Senecan monologue by Areus breaks Octavius to announce the rout and death of Brutus. The ensuing dialogue of balanced contrasts passes to Senecan speeches. After a chorus Antony vaunts the deeds of his mythical ancestors and his own prowess. The only function of Ventidius is to listen. Antony, Octavius, and Lepidus, in balanced dialogue, then in longer speeches, agree to divide the world. The chorus of soldiers rejoices in the prospect of booty.

Act IV brings the rout and death of Brutus to Portia by messenger. Her long tirades culminate in her speech on receiving the urn of ashes, and are followed by a chorus.

Act V is an epilogue. The Nurse reports the death of Portia, and engages in responsive lyrics with the chorus of soldiers.

Not really five acts, then, but three frame a piece without dramatic action. Though it is focused on a brief period, it does not thereby realize dramatic sequence. Consisting of oratory and lyric, it is conceived as a poem, not as a play.

The style, careful in the balances of the dialogue, has effective oratorical iteration: "C'est trop, c'est trop duré, c'est trop acquis."

Jupiter, qui *voit tout, voit* bien qu'il ne te reste
Pour avoir *tout* ce *rond* que la *rondeur* céleste.
Il ha peur pour soymesme, *il hi peur* que tes bras . . .
                                            (I. 21).

The more pervasive suggestion of internal rhyme is combined with this again in the fifth act.

Or' il est *temps* d'*ouv*rir la p*orte*;
Il est t*emps* de m*our*ir, lang*our*euse vieillesse,
Vieillesse lang*our*euse, hélas! qu'att*ens*-tu plus? (V. 82).

Of the same type are the two tragedies of 1574,
Hippolyte and *Cornélie.*

Act I of *Cornélie* is again a prelude consisting of a fine
monologue and a chorus. In II Cornelia and Cicero remind
each other of the past and moralize on human life. The
theme of mutability, carried out in the chorus, ends on the
hope of another deliverance from tyrants. In III the chorus
continues this theme after dialogue with Cornelia and her
receiving of Pompey's ashes. IV brings on first Cassius and
Brutus, then Caesar and Antony. V, though more nearly an
act, makes extravagant use of the messenger.

Marc-Antoine (1578), surer perhaps in its oratory and
finer in its lyric, is no more dramatic.

Philostratus, a minor person, is added (II. i) merely to expound the situation in a monologue. Octavius and Agrippa
appear only in IV. Lucilius is in III only to receive the exhalations of Antony; and Charmion has little more function
in II and V. Once more V is mainly a series of tirades. Act
II, scene iii adds to Cleopatra's oratory a flash of jealousy
and the suggestion of Diomedes that she save the situation
by using her fatal beauty on Caesar; but neither is carried out.

In *La Troade* (1579) Garnier turned to Euripides.

Act I, for the first time more than a prelude, consists nevertheless, after Hecuba's opening monologue, of responsive
lyrics between her and the chorus. The envoy Talthybius arrives toward the end. Act II, mainly a debate between Andromache and Ulysses, introduces Helen and Astyanax and
closes with a chorus. Act III, bringing back Hecuba and
Talthybius, adds Pyrrhe, Agamemnon, Calchas, and Polyxena.
Act IV brings together Hecuba and Andromache. The murder
of Astyanax and the death, already forecast, of Polyxena are
announced by messenger. Act V gives main place to Poly-
mestor, who appears for the first time. The act is in effect
an appendix, adding the *Hecuba* of Euripides to Seneca.

Evidently Garnier has not grasped the composing habit
of Greek tragedy. At most he has managed somewhat
more interaction between such groups of persons as he
had begun by keeping apart in separate acts. He is working at literature, not at drama. Hence his evident intelligence carries his experience only so far. The argument of
Antigone (1580) cites the Theban plays of all three
great Greek dramatists, and adds Statius to Seneca. The
plot generally uses Seneca for the first three acts, the
Antigone of Sophocles for the last two. The combination
is rather piecing than fusion, and shows no appreciation
of the dramaturgy of Sophocles. In 1582 Garnier was
adventurous enough to attempt a dramatization of Ariosto.
Bradamante, which he calls a tragicomedy,[5] is hardly
more than a division of certain parts of the *Orlando* into
scenes which are far from being dramatic units. As in the
earlier plays, the five acts are in effect three. Some char-

[5] On tragicomedy, see H. C. Lancaster, *The French Tragicomedy,
Its Origins and Development from 1552 to 1628* (Baltimore, 1907).

acterization is achieved in the minor persons Aymon and Beatrix. Bradamante herself is chosen, of course, for those lyric tirades with which Ariosto had delighted the century.

But Garnier lived to vindicate tragedy within his own limits. *Les Juifves* (1583) has more values for representation and, in the pervasive suggestion of the inextinguishable mission of Israel, a certain unity of tone. "The subject is taken," says the argument, "from the 24th and 25th chapters of the fourth book of Kings, the 36th chapter of the second book of Chronicles, and the 29th chapter of Jeremiah, and is more amply treated by Josephus in the 9th and 10th chapters of his Antiquities."

The persons are the Prophet, Nebuchadnezzar, Nabuz, and Amital; the Jewish Queens and Nebuchadnezzar's Queen; a Duenna and a Provost; and the frequently appearing Chorus. Two other main persons, Zedekiah and the High Priest, appear first in IV; the Prophet, only in I and V. As in the earlier tragedies, I is a monologue of lamentation on the Captivity plus a chorus, that is, an expository prelude; and V, reporting the slaughter of the children, is an epilogue urging submission to the will of God and the hope of deliverance by Cyrus. Though the groups are somewhat better combined, there is little change in the habit of composition.

Such effectiveness as this tragedy has beyond spectacle is mainly lyric. The abundant choruses and responses are both expert as verse and inspired by Psalms and Prophets to eloquence: Adieu, native land (II. v); How shall we sing in a strange land? (III. iii); Wretched daughters of

Sion (IV. i). Though there is some interaction of plea and refusal, some suspense, all the decisions have been made beforehand. There remain to animate a play the sight and sound of communal fortitude. *Les Juifves* is a noble poem; its literary type is still clear in the nobler *Samson Agonistes* of Milton.

That Garnier's classicism is thoroughly of his time is vouched by forty editions in less than thirty years. He was classical superficially in following the custom of mythological ornament. He was classical further in imitations on classical themes with classical persons, and still further in going from Seneca to Euripides and even to Sophocles. But his classicism kept sixteenth-century limits in looking away from composition to style. As to the Middle Age, dramatic meant to his time not a distinctive movement, but a certain style. Though he was intelligent and serious enough to use Seneca in his own way, less than the Elizabethans for melodrama, more for moral urgency, he did not see beyond the Senecan conception of drama as oratory plus lyric. He found his own oratory, his own lyric; but his progress was rather in tragic diction than in tragedy.[6]

3. HISTORY PLAYS

The most distinctive Elizabethan stage experiments of the waning sixteenth century were the "histories." Generally lacking focus, series rather than sequence, often made over, sometimes nationalistic propaganda, they still keep some of their Elizabethan stir. For the putting of

[6] For Garnier in England, see A. M. Witherspoon, *The Influence of Robert Garnier on Elizabethan Drama* (New Haven, 1924).

great men on the stage not only satisfied a story appetite growing too fast for print; it showed prowess, as no story can quite show, in action. Thus a history play, though it might be tragedy only in the medieval sense of the fall of a prince, though it might be Senecan enough in style, might teach stage values beyond Seneca. Widening the field of tragedy beyond Greek legend to the opening East and to national history, it also opened other methods of characterization and other dramatic forms than were taught by either the Greek or the Latin tradition.

The story play, then, should not be ruled out as *a priori* undramatic. Aristotelian theory and classical experience exhibit dramatic movement as typically distinct from narrative, not the telling of the story, but the compelling of its crisis to an emotional issue. In this aspect the Greek tragic theater exhibits sharp contrasts to the Elizabethan: the one vast, open, removing the audience so far as to compel orotund delivery and preclude facial expression, the other small, closed, bringing the audience so near as to invite facial play and even aside; the one limited to a few persons, the other inviting many; the one unifying plot for the sake of unbroken, cumulative sequence to an inevitable issue, the other dispersing it over time and space for narrative values and for individualizing characterization; the one crisis play, the other story play. But the contrast is not absolute, nor does it establish exclusive superiority. Greek tragedy is too great in its kind to need any cult of it as the *beau idéal*. The sixteenth century might have progressed faster for understanding that dramaturgy; but Shakspere came before Corneille and by another road. Elizabethan drama, often bungling, sometimes sprawling at first, and slow to master the essentially dramatic method of interaction, was yet a school of various experience. Though the experience of the "histories" was valuable mainly as preparatory, it also vindicated the dramatic validity of a story play.

Marlowe's *Tamburlaine* (1587) is poetry not only in what the Middle Age called high style, but in dramatic conception. Though his sequel failed to make it a tragedy, it is history brought home in heroic action. The fourth act, indeed, lapses into spectacle; the fifth pushes the ruthlessness beyond credibility, and the close is a formal gesture; but for three acts we are in the thick. Not sustained as a sequence, this activity is nevertheless dramatic to the extent of being typically distinct from Seneca. For all its oratory, *Tamburlaine* is story in action. Thus was opened the way for Shakspere's "histories" of the 90's. We shall do his revolting *Richard III* more justice if we neither excuse it as carrying over an earlier appeal of blood, nor blame it for failing to focus the monster in a tragedy. *Richard III* is not tragedy dulled by dispersion; it is dramatic story, dramatic in the interactions of that princely world poisoned by treachery, story in cumulative damnation. Shakspere had written the *Merchant of Venice* and was writing *As You Like It,* when he put on another "history" in *Henry V* (1599).

4. PASTORAL AND RUSTIC COMEDY

Before the dramatic experience of the "histories" bore its best fruit in a widening of tragedy, another sort of story enriched comedy. Dramatic training through Latin comedy had been continuous from the Middle Age through the Renaissance. As Ariosto had begun with *I suppositi* in 1509, so Shakspere wrote the *Comedy of Errors* in 1591. In Latin and in vernacular, in translation and in imitation, the quick, smart formula of Plautus and Terence[7] continued its lessons. But the abundant Renaissance pageantry of solemn entries, the court shows, and the vogue of pastoral, had yielded here and there some dramatic experience. This is evident as early as Poliziano,[8] whose *Orfeo* is classical in its pagan gods and demigods, specifically pastoral in its shepherds. It is also myth, both in the original story of Orpheus and Eurydice and in Poliziano's shaping. His myth is effective spectacle; his dialogue more than conventional responses. He has action enough to conclude upon vociferous melodrama. *Orfeo* is a play so far as it goes; but it is too brief to make its dramatic sequence convincing. Mythological drama is rather opened than established. In 1573 Tasso, fulfilling a similar commission for a court show at Urbino, conformed his *Aminta*[9] strictly to unity of place and time. But its sequence, though uninterrupted, is hardly dramatic. It proceeds oftener by musical recitative than by action.

[7] For Plautus and Terence, see ARP.

[8] "Politian was in 1471, at the request of Cardinal Francesco Gonzaga, despatched to Mantua by Lorenzo de' Medici to prepare an entertainment for the reception of Duke Galeazzo Maria Sforza. The *Orfeo*, a lyric pastoral in dramatic form, prophetic of so much that was later to come, was the contribution of the brilliant humanist and poet to the Duke's entertainment. It stands close to the fountainhead of European secular drama." H. M. Ayres, preface to his translation of the *Orfeo* in *Romanic Review*, XX (January, 1929), 1.

[9] See Chapter IV.

Lovely to see and hear, it gives more hints for opera than for drama. Battista Guarini (1538–1612), professor of rhetoric and poetic at Ferrara, and chief court poet after the withdrawal of Tasso, spent years on his pastoral drama *Il pastor fido*.

Begun in 1580, finished in 1583, read aloud, revised, it was finally published at Venice 1589/90. Apparently it was first staged in 1595. The Venice edition of 1602 is the twentieth. Called tragicomedy, tragedy in its crisis of life and death, comedy in its satyr and in its happy issue, it is above all, in its persons, its scene, its mythology, consistently pastoral. A prologue celebrating Arcadia as a blest retreat of peace, and Caterina d'Este as worthy of her illustrious house, is spoken by the river Alfeo. Besides this personification, and four choruses, there are eighteen personae. Of these the majority are servants or companions serving merely as interlocutors. Three, the temple officiant Nicander, Corisca's lover Corydon, and a messenger, are quite superfluous. No person is characterized except as a type: the hero Mirtillo as a devotedly faithful lover, the heroine Amaryllis as virtuous, Corisca as a plotter. All are duly paganized.

I. The plays opens with old Linco's advice to athletic young Silvio: go love betimes. A dialogue between Mirtillo expounds the plot. Corisca's monologue tells the audience that she is in love with Mirtillo, and must have revenge for his disdain. Three elders, Tityrus, the priest Montano, and Dameta, further expound the situation in reminiscence. A satyr, in a monologue on love, vows to seize the tricky Corisca. The persons having been thus presented in separate sets, the act ends with a chorus.

II. Mirtillo tells Ergasto how he fell in love forever with Amaryllis. Dorinda in vain woos Silvio by detaining and restoring his hound. Corisca's monologue exults in the outlook of her plot, and her dialogue misleading Amaryllis ends with soliloquy. The satyr seizing her, she cajoles, insults, and finally breaks away, thus providing action for the first time. The concluding chorus moralizes the past.

III. Mirtillo, after apostrophizing spring and love, is brought, through a game of nymphs devised by Corisca, to Amaryllis, declares his passion, exchanges longer and longer speeches, and finding her obdurate, vows to die. In a monologue she tells the audience that she loves him nevertheless. Corisca tricks them separately into seeking a cave. Each exhales a monologue on the way. This is the complication. The satyr unwittingly furthers it by blocking the cave with a rock, thus imprisoning the two innocents. The chorus meditates on love.

IV. At this point all that remains of the action is to disclose Corisca's trick, correct the mistaken identity, and reveal the true intent of the oracle. But since the play must have five acts Guarini reserves all this to V, and makes IV a stalling interlude of monologues, reports, and choruses. The only action is in the last scene (ix), where Silvio, accidentally wounding Dorinda, begins to fall in love with her.

V. Mirtillo's foster-father, arriving from far, finds him about to be sacrificed, having offered himself in place of Amaryllis. The disclosure that these two are the fated couple meant by the oracle is made gradually through five scenes, and capped by the arrival of the blind seer Tirenio in vi. Silvio is reported duly in love with the healed Dorinda. Even Corisca is pardoned; and the play ends with hymeneal choruses.

The play is not moved by the actions of its persons. Complication, indeed, comes through Corisca, who is the only person carried through the play; but the solution is through persons brought in at the end solely for that purpose. As with Garnier, the persons are presented in separate groups; and they are on the stage to talk. The style is expertly careful. Guarini has learned from Tasso how to modulate his verse. The notes record constant reminiscences of the classics, both Greek and Latin, and many borrowings; but the surcharging, again after the example of Tasso, is discreetly harmonized. Pastoral drama, then, rather prolonged pastoral than advanced drama. But its opportunities for spectacle, dance, music, and imaginative suggestion were among the motives finally woven into a play by Shakspere.

Meantime real rustics also, actual farmers, laborers, villagers, had long been dramatized for gentlefolk and bourgeois by amateurs and increasingly by professional companies. Angelo Beolco (1502–1542), called from one of his favorite impersonations Ruzzante, even localized them on the stage in Ferrara and Venice by Paduan dialect. As the shepherds of the Towneley *Secunda pastorum,* his rustics are presented realistically. Here is the essential difference from pastoral. The actual rudeness of such impersonations, may, indeed, be dramatically exaggerated; but it must always seem actual. Ruzzante's vivid realizations transcend his Paduan dialect by the appeal of actual peasant life, rudeness, shrewdness, lewdness unveiled by the social conventions of a higher society, talking in their own terms. Such rustic drama in time helped to discover a dramatic interest beyond types in individuals. Types remain useful in comedy because they are readily recognizable, the braggart soldier or the clever rascal; and dramatic theory urges nothing more. But the stage attempts with rustic persons sometimes opened in comedy of manners the further appeal of characterization. The verisimilitude and propriety of the theorists gave way to dramatic creation. As later in the "histories," so in rustic comedies, theory was widened by stage experience.

Ruzzante's life was too short to bring his art to maturity. At forty, though he had already triumphed in single characterizations, he was still groping in the forms of Plautus. Much of his work is what is now called sketch, rather dialogue or even monologue than play.

A characteristic piece is his *First Dialogue.* A soldier, reminiscent here and elsewhere of the *miles gloriosus,* but characterized with some individuality, is returning from the war ragged and wistful, but still boastful. Catechized by an old friend, he gives his experiences, his theory of life, and something of himself. So far the form is hardly more than monologue; for the friend merely listens, questions, and comments. There is no interaction. The effect, however, even in print, is dramatic to the extent of vivid representation. The racy language has constant suggestions of manner, gesture, stage business. It differs essentially from the diction of Garnier. We come to know this man.

Then the soldier meets his wife. She is interested, not moved. Having had to shift for herself in his absence, she cannot now break off convenient relations for sentiment. Here is interaction, even a situation, and the lines given to the man and to the woman clearly suggest it; but more than lines are needed to make it a play. So

Ruzzante took this second part for the motive of his *Second Dialogue*. He saw the situation; he gave it some complication, and closed upon violent action; but he did not sustain the interaction of man and woman, and his third person, her senile lover, remains almost separate.

So Ruzzante's collected pieces[10] generally show less achievement than promise. He was learning rapidly from the stage itself. Imperfect playwright at his untimely death, he was already famous as a writer and actor of "parts." These Italian stage experiments of the 1530's were essentially like the Elizabethan fifty years later in giving to an old field new stage values. Though they had rather a local success than any general influence, they are significant now for what they opened.

In 1586 John Lyly gave the persons of his *Endymion* Greek or Latin names. But the myth suggested by his title does not take shape as plot. Indeed, there is hardly any action, none that is dramatically determining. The persons are on the stage to talk, the main persons in orations, the Latin-comedy servants in repartee. Endymion's dream is presented by a dumb show in Act II, and recounted in Act IV. The close is flatly by Cynthia's fiat. The allegory, clearer of course to the audience than to us, seems to be both personification of qualities and suggestion of actual persons, as in Spenser's *Faerie Queene*. In both aspects it now makes a dull play duller.

Peele's *Old Wives' Tale* is as random as its title, adding rustics to classics and allegory to folklore. Not a story

---

[10] Alfred Mortier, *Un Dramaturge populaire . . . Ruzzante.* Œuvres compl. traduites pour la première fois (Paris, 1926).

play, it is a collection of little shows, each rather for itself than for any sequence. The folklore material and the rustics are interesting; the play is not. That anything so shapeless could have gained the stage in 1590 is sufficient evidence of Elizabethan willingness to experiment. Within five years Shakspere found the dramatic solution of myth and pastoral, folklore and rustics, for court show in the *Midsummer Night's Dream*. Forthwith Lyly's pedantic encomium and clumsy dumb show, Peele's jolly rustics and half-fairies, become as antiquated as the many Elizabethan gropings through the moralities and pastoral. The court show has arrived at fairyland. For this is all faery: the ancient heroic world from Boccaccio and Chaucer, and the sprites with classical names. The classical story of Pyramus and Thisbe is transmitted by rustics; and Bottom himself is translated. Through all hovers the authentic elfin minister Puck.

Midsummer Night's Dream is a complete fusion, not only of style as Tasso's *Aminta,* but also in dramatic movement. As Theseus, Puck, and Bottom, the lovers and yokels, are all conformed to the same world, so they all interact in a single sequence toward a uniting issue. Even the place is single. Such slight shifts as there may have been in the Elizabethan theater are negligible; for of all its many presentations the most convincing have stayed on a lawn before a green thicket. *Midsummer Night's Dream* is a one-act play, Greek dramaturgy beyond Garnier's or Tasso's. But instead of saying that Shakspere conformed to the dramatic unities, we should rather say that he learned the dramatic importance of holding fairyland together. Sixteenth-century stage experience, then, as well as classical theory and imitation, opened the great drama of the seventeenth century. The experience of court shows with the feebleness of allegory, the escape of pastoral, the vitality of rustic realism, opened the way for both romantic and realistic comedy. The experience of the "histories" opened a new appeal in tragedy. For Corneille, as well as Shakspere, was a man of the stage.

Chapter VII

SIXTEENTH-CENTURY POETICS

THE revival of classical Latin was promoted by manuals and discussions, and accompanied by still others directed to vernacular poetry. Though none of these ranks as a poetic in the sense of a contribution to the theory of poetry, not a few reveal or define habits of thought and taste, directions of study, literary ideals and methods. Thus their importance, far beyond their intrinsic values, is in their clues to literary preoccupations and trends, their indications for a Renaissance weather map.

1. VIDA

The ecclesiastic, Marco Girolamo Vida, addressed his three cantos of Latin hexameters *De arte poetica* (1527) to the Dauphin, son of Francis I, with due invocation of the Muses.

> Sit fas vestra mihi vulgare arcana per orbem,
> Pierides, penitusque sacros recludere fontes,
> Dum vatem egregium teneris educere ab annis,
> Heroum qui facta canet, laudesve deorum,
> Mentem agito, vestrique in vertice sistere montis.

It invites noble youth to write Latin poetry. The doctrine is mainly an expansion of the "Ars poetica" of Horace;[1] the exemplar is Vergil.

[1] ARP and MRP.

I. Though heroic poetry is the highest, choose according to your talent heroic or dramatic, elegiac or pastoral. Let the great work wait while you sound and explore it; but meantime seize those parts that come at once, and make a prose sketch of the whole. The preparation of schooling in poetic and rhetoric is necessary as training in appreciation. [The rest of the canto is addressed, over the pupil's shoulder, to teachers.] Greek, established in Italy by the Medici, and especially Homer, stimulate comparison. Of the Latins, the Augustans, especially Vergil, have first claim. The others may wait till taste has been matured by these. The master's function is to awaken and guide love of the best poetry without forcing it. Even recreation may be pointed by classical suggestions. Calf love must be handled with care. So soon as young ardor has penetrated through passion to poetry, the boy should study its monuments and taste the other arts. Though travel is useful, and some experience of war, the central thing is unremitting study of the poets. Thus metric, instead of remaining merely a set of rules, becomes the testing of one's own adjustments by memories of reading, the oral revision of a mind full of great poetry. Young ambitions should not be quelled by too severe criticism, nor lack the privilege of retirement and freedom. The world that grudges these owes its glory nevertheless to poets, who have sacrificed worldly rewards to live in their own peace. As the fire stolen by Prometheus, poetry is a divine gift.

II. The second canto repeats Horace's counsel: begin on a subdued tone and at the crisis (*in mediis*). The action, planned as a whole and clearly forecast, should control the description. Greek is more tolerant of descriptive dilation than is becoming to us Latins. Need I caution against the dilation that comes from gratuitous display of erudition? The detail of Vulcan's shield for Aeneas has the point of exhibiting the history of Rome. Variety has its claims; but rolls of kings, legends, myths, comic relief, though delightful as description, should not deviate. Be careful of verisimilitude. Do not plan for length. Work day and night on a conception limited and tried out this way and that. If amplification seems desirable afterward, Vergil shows many ways. [The citations are mainly descriptive.] Inspiration comes when it will, and does not obviate revision. Study nature: the ways of age, of youth, of woman, of servants and of kings, for appropriateness, as in Vergil; for so you learn to move, as Vergil by Euryalus. Study in others, especially in the ancient Greeks, their conceptions (*inventa*) without hesitating to borrow as Vergil from Homer. So may Rome ever excel in the arts and teach the world. Alas for our discords and the bringing in of foreign tyrants! though distant nations had already honored Tuscan Leo and the Medici. The crusade against the Saracens became only a dream.

III. Flee obscurity; let poetry be clear in its own light. Vary to avoid repetition. Figures give vividness to both poetry and oratory; but verse is freer with hyperbole, metonymy, personification. Figures should avoid display, incongruity, dilation. Style must always be appropriate. Follow the classics, use suggestions from other poets, adapting the old to the new, even borrowing. As a poet need not fear new words that are already recognizable, so he may go to Greek, as his classical ancestors before him. He may venture cautiously on archaism, periphrasis, compounds, adaptations. Never let words carry you beyond your meaning, except to serve the music of verse. Verse is a shrine closed to the mass of men, open to the few by a narrow way. For it must range beyond mere correctness to harmony with the persons, with the scene, with each of the three styles. Such counsels, sure as they are, will not guarantee high achievement. That can be given only by Apollo. Let us close by celebrating the supreme poet Vergil.

Commonplaces of rhetoric, from a source commonplace for centuries, why were these put into elegant Vergilian hexameters? Hardly to make the Dauphin a Latin poet; hardly to interpret what was already too well known; hardly to advance poetic. The poem is an exhibition of competence in learning, in teaching, and in Latin verse, a sort of thesis for the degree of humanist. The person that it seeks to establish as a Latin poet is its author.

2. TRISSINO

The seven divisions of poetic (1529, enlarged 1563) by Giovan Giorgio Trissino occupy the first 139 pages of the second volume of his collected works (Verona, 1729). The first four divisions are devoted to diction, metric, and verse forms. The fifth and sixth are substantially an Italian paraphrase of Aristotle's *Poetic*[2] with insertions from the "Ars poetica" of Horace. Trissino repeats Aristotle without grasp of his distinctive ideas. He has read also Dionysius of Halicarnassus (105); he has the independence to disparage Seneca (101); and he considers why Dante called his great work *Commedia* (120); but he thinks that pastoral eclogue is of the same poetic genus as comedy, and he does not make clear that Aristotle's distinction of dramatic from epic is in composition. Though Trissino had not penetration enough to be constructive, or even suggestive, he opened Aristotle early in the century to the wider circle.

3. GIRALDI CINTHIO

Giraldi Cinthio published together two essays on the composition of romances,[3] comedies, and tragedies (*Dis-*

---

[2] For Aristotle's *Poetic,* see ARP.
[3] For discussion of the romances, see Chapter V. For Giraldi's *novelle,* see Chapter VIII, I, c.

corsi . . . intorno al comporre de i romanzi, delle commedie, e delle tragedie . . . Venice, 1554). In the one on comedy and tragedy (pages 199–287, written in 1543) he moves, as Trissino, over the surface of Aristotle's *Poetic* without grasping the import of poetic as a distinct form of composition. For style he even prefers Seneca (220) to the Greeks. In the essay on verse romances (pages 1–198, written in 1549) he speaks of having presented the subject in oral teaching, and refers (4) to Vicentio Maggio's lectures on Aristotle.

The word *romance* has the same meaning with us as epic with the Romans (5); and the form originated in France (6). Considering first the plot (*favola*), as Aristotle bids, we see in Boiardo and Ariosto that romance is the adorning (*abbellimento*) of the strife of Christians with their enemies (9). Though thus like epic or tragedy in imitating illustrious deeds, romance has not a single action (12), but several, perhaps eight or ten. Its organization (*orditura*) is unhappily compared to that of the human body: the subject being the skeleton; the order of parts, the nerves; the beautification, the skin; the animation, the soul. This is the plan of the treatise.

A single action is too restrictive for romance (22), whose many actions are more desirable, as conducive to variety (25). But the actions should be connected in a continuous chain (*continua catena*) and have verisimilitude. The parts should cohere as the parts of the human body. The poem should be fleshed out at suitable places (26) with fillings (*riempimenti*): loves, hates, laments, descriptions of places, of seasons, of persons, tales made up or taken from the ancients, voyages, wanderings, marvels [in short, anything for sophistic display]. For there is nothing in heaven above, nor in the earth beneath, nor in the very depth of the abyss, which is not at the call of the judicious poet—provided (27) each be appropriate in itself and to the whole.

The appended proviso is irrelevant in theory and was not observed in practice. The age of classicism is faced with the fact that its most evident and most popular poetic achievement is not classical in composition. Renaissance romance does not follow the epic formula. True, Ariosto does begin *in mediis rebus* (23), as Horace bids; but even that is not obligatory for a "manifold action"; and evidently the action may be not merely manifold, but plural. By "continuous chain" Giraldi means not sequence of the whole, but merely transitions; not connection, but connectives (40, 41).

Our romancers may have learned this from Claudian (41). The breaking off of an action creates suspense; and the main stories remain in suspense to the completion of the whole poem (42). Besides, variety is itself an added beauty. Why must romances be limited to the epic way (44)? Ovid did not follow Vergil (45). But the parts and the episodes must have the connection of verisimilitude (55).

It seems difficult for Giraldi to think in terms of composition. Once more we arrive at verisimilitude; and we go on to appropriateness (*il decoro*).

This he has touched earlier in reprehending Homer (31) for letting Nausicaa wash clothes. Here (63–65) he insists that romance, in bringing on kings as well as shepherds and nymphs, must make each consistent with his type. After pausing to disagree with the Italian followers of Hermogenes, he passes to style (83–159), including verse. The section on verse, sometimes dubious, is often suggestive, as on Ariosto's admirable facility (145) in making verse run as easily as prose [i.e., without inversions]. Petrarch is cited (147) as the ideal combination of weight and ease.

The concluding section (160–184) on the soul of the poem manages to lean even more on rhetoric. In oratory *anima* depends on delivery; in poetry, not only on this, but on such expressive words as put things before our eyes (*energia, sotto gli occhi*). An appendix (188–197) repeats the Horatian counsels on advice and revision.

The main significance of the treatise in 1549 is its recognition of the actual difference of romance from epic. Giraldi's attempts at reconciling the two in theory seem evasions because he misses Aristotle's controlling view of poetic as having its own ways of sequence, distinct from those of rhetoric.

4. MUZIO

Muzio published among his Italian poems a poetic in verse (*Rime diverse del Mutio Iustinopolitano: tre libri di arte poetica . . .* Venice, 1551). Diffused through some 1,600 lines (pages 68–94), it is often thin and sometimes vague, the sort of treatise written not to teach, nor much to theorize, but to express the author's culture and taste via Horace's "Ars poetica." What individuality it has transpires for the most part incidentally; but the treatment of metric is fairly distinctive.

Why use Greek terms: ode, hymn, epigram, elegy (71*)? Why talk of dactyls and spondees (72)? The difference between quantitative and accentual verse forbids the transfer. You will make a hodgepodge like Coccai's.

> Non puote orecchie haver giudicio saldo
> Di quantità & di tempo ove la lingua
> De l'accente conviene esser seguace. (72*)

"The ear cannot respond surely to quantity and time where the tongue must follow the stress" is at once penetrative and, in the face of the classicists, daring. After conventional remarks on verse as expressing that harmony which in nature we see to be divine, and on the ancient relation to the dance, he finds the joining of lyre with song in *ottava rima* (77) and in *stanza* (86). The Greeks and Romans, using hexameter for all "three styles," did not even adapt their verse to tragedy or to comedy (88*) by the length of the line. Our unrhymed verse (*versi sciolti*) is appropriate to proud and lofty emprise (88*). For purity of style it is not enough to be born in Tuscany. Seek usage in books (70*). Tuscan is not confined to Petrarch. He was pure and fluent above all others— and perhaps more timid than becomes a poet (71).

The treatment of imitation (69*, 70, 82) and of sentences (68*, 90*, 91, 93) is conventional. Sophistic appears in the recipes for verisimilitude through appropriateness (77–78) and in the recommendation of showpieces (Aetna, winter, spring, etc. 83). But Muzio at once makes a significant addition. "You might yourself look at nature, not merely seek it in books. Learn what to dilate, what to compress." As examples of the force of restraint (84) he cites Vergil's mating of Dido and Aeneas in the cave and Dante's Paolo and Francesca.

5. FRACASTORO

A Latin dialogue (1555) by Girolamo Fracastoro discusses poetry as a form of eloquence, merging poetic in rhetoric (*Hieronymi Fracastorii Naugerius sive de poetica dialogus* . . . with an English translation by Ruth Kelso and an introduction by Murray W. Bundy, University of

Illinois Press, 1924). Ciceronian in type, it is clearly ordered and composed, and agreeably fluent in style. Fracastoro's motive is not professional. Scientist and philosopher, he turns to poetry as to an important item in culture and a suggestive topic for discussion. So approached by not a few Renaissance scholars, it imposed no obligation to advance critical theory.

6. PELETIER

L'Art poétique of Jacques Peletier du Mans is a similar excursion of a scholar into literature. Philosopher and mathematician as Fracastoro, interested in languages, professor, promoter of normalized spelling, he was known, by that adjective dear to the French Renaissance, as "docte Peletier." His literary associations were first with Ronsard and Du Bellay under Jean Dorat at the Collège de Coqueret; later he had associations in Lyon, where Jean de Tournes published his treatise in 1555 (*L'art poëtique* . . . publié d'après l'édition unique avec introduction et commentaire [par] André Boulanger, Paris, 1930).

His editor, regarding it as the best formulation of the Pléiade movement, notes that it relies on Horace's "Ars poetica" [which Peletier had translated ten years before], Cicero, and Quintilian, that it uses no Greek source and of the Italians only Vida, that the great model is Vergil, and that the section on dramaturgy is slight and feeble. He sums up the doctrine as: (1) use your vernacular and enrich it; (2) imitate the ancients; (3) imitate nature; (4) cultivate the high poetic forms urged by the Pléiade.

The little that Peletier has to say on poetic composition is all rhetoric. He makes, for example, the usual transfer of the counsels for *exordium* to the opening of a poem. He shows the sophistic slant in turning to encomium the Horatian commonplace that poets are givers of fame (71, 82, 89, 176) and in the stock show-pieces (127). He is more distinctive on rhyme (149), on classification of meters by the number of syllables (153), and on imitation of classical verse forms (159). He occasionally cites Ariosto (103, 201) and discusses both the sonnet and the ode (169, 172).

7. MINTURNO

Minturno made his more comprehensive and influential Latin dialogue on classical poetic, *De poeta,* a collection of six monologues, or essays, with enough question and objection for occasional reminder of the literary form, but with little real discussion (*Antonii Sebastiani Minturni de poeta . . . libri sex,* Venice, 1559). The setting, a villa by the sea, is elaborately described in the introduction. The style, oratorical and inclined to Ciceronianism, is throughout elaborate and diffuse, each noun being habitually escorted by two adjectives. What is thus conveyed with much repetition is generally Horace's "Ars poetica" once more, Cicero, and Quintilian; but there is also considerable use, though little comprehension, of Aristotle's *Poetic.* Aristotle's conception of poetry as a distinct kind of composition has not yet arrived; and poetic style, which is Minturno's actual subject, is conceived in the terms of rhetoric. The spokesmen are: Book

I Sincerus (Sannazaro) on What is poetry?; Book II Pontanus (recalled, not present) on What is poetic?; Book III Vopiscus on tragedy; Book IV Gauricus on comedy; Book V Carbo on lyric; Book VI Sincerus on style. The quotations adduced on the first two hundred pages show the following proportions: Vergil above all (*Bucolics,* 55 lines; *Georgics,* 10 lines; *Aeneid,* 512 lines); Seneca, 101; Horace (mainly "Ars poetica"), 99; Euripides (in Latin), 68; Sophocles (in Latin), 23.

I. What is poetry? It is a *furor coelestis.* Wisdom and eloquence being one, all who had it used to be called poets (Moses, Theseus, Lycurgus, Solon); for poetry was the only art of speech. Recovering now from medieval darkness, we see Vergil as the exemplar of everything, Homer as comprehending all philosophy. Poetry is imitation of nature [apparently conceived as description]. Therefore Plato's exclusion is rejected. The imitation is narrative in epic, through *personae* in dramatic poetry, and a combination of the two in melic. That poetry is like painting (Horace's "ut pictura poesis") is agreed. Poets seek variety rather than sequence, and prefer violent or otherwise disturbed states of mind, considering the [rhetorical] headings of appropriateness to habit, place, and time. Plato's preference of epic is approved against Aristotle's of tragedy.

II. What is poetic? [The implication of this book, as throughout, is that poetic is rhetoric.] The ancient poets thought their distinction to be not in verse, but in lore of astronomy, optics, music, logic, history, geography. In *ratio dicendi* historians are likest to poets. Vergil was expert in rhetoric and logic as well as in cosmogony, morals, law and polity, medicine, athletics, etc. Poetry belongs under *ratio civilis.* Its object is to teach, to delight, to move [the stock summary for oratory]. It must command the "three styles" in order to be always appropriate. The natural objection of Traianus that this seems to be all rhetoric is answered by citing the distinction of verse, by slipping back to the "three styles," and, as in a sort of desperation, by saying that the poet's distinctive gift is to move men to wonder (*admiratio*). [Not only is this pure sophistic, but Minturno's floundering is due to his seeing no distinction at all. He always falls back on rhetoric.] The poet, no less than the orator, must command *inventio, dispositio, elocutio, memoria, pronuntiatio.* Tragedy is discussed as a poem with parts like those of a speech and with descriptive amplification. Its *personae* are to be fashioned through the headings of rhetoric. "The other parts of an oration with which the orator is concerned, division, confirmation, rebuttal, conclusion, peroration, must also be observed (*tenendae*) by the poet."

A book inquiring what poetic is, including tragedy, and quoting Aristotle, has not the faintest suggestion of a distinctive poetic composition! It can translate Aristotle's complication and solution without seeing that his mainspring is sequence, and consider his "recognition" as a means of display.

Once more we are told that characterization must be true in the sense of being true to type: Aeneas consistently *pius et fortis,* Achilles *iracundus et magnanimus,* Ulysses *prudens et callidus,* according to the headings of rhetoric. After a few vague precepts on arrangement, and one more reminder of the "three styles," a close is at last found in the epic eminence of Vergil.

III. (Tragedy) is again conventional. With little use of Aristotle, it reverts to Horace and Seneca, and repeats the rhetorical doctrine of types. Tragedy is found to consist of plot, character, words, and pregnant sentences (*fabula, mores, verba, sententiae*). Its externals are described, its parts enumerated, its origin summarized. It should have five acts of not more than ten scenes each. Its style should be graphically vivid. [To this counsel of rhetoric, which applies to drama only in the reports of messengers, no hint is added of the distinctive quality of dramatic dialogue.]

IV. (Comedy) after a review of the history of comedy and an enumeration of its typical *personae,* is devoted largely to a long list of figures used for comic effect, and closes with enumeration of its parts.

V. (Lyric) after a long introduction on *convivium,* with quotations from the poets, distinguishes melic from dithyrambic and nomic, and finds that lyric has as many components as drama (*fabula, mores, verba, sententiae!*). Its forms are ode (with epode and palinode), satiric iambs, elegy (nenia, epicedium, epitaphium, epithanatium), epigram in the Greek sense, and satire.

VI. (Style) is a summary of the section on style in any classical rhetoric, with classified examples and with the usual lists of figures.

What is the result of these 570 pages? Five men of letters, besides the author, have roles in a sort of published academy; and several others at least take a hand. They have no new ideas, except certain Aristotelian inklings that hardly seem to fit. But they are learned in rhetoric. They begin with the convention of the original dominance of poetry; they end with sixty-two figures of speech. The subject is reviewed; it is not advanced. As guidance for Latin poets—but that is hardly intended. As inspiration this oratory is much feebler than Poliziano's; and it never even approaches that brief, anonymous ancient prose poem περι ὕψους, *De sublimitate,* "on reaching up."[4]

[4] ARP.

Minturno's other treatise, *Arte poetica* (1563), reduces the dialogue form to catechism (*L'arte poetica del signor Antonio Minturno, nella quale si contengono i precetti eroici, tragici, comici, satirici* . . . Naples, 1725). Though there is some debate in Book I on the validity of *romanzo* narrative, elsewhere the single interlocutor assigned to each book merely asks the right questions. The work is not a discussion; it is a manual of vernacular poetry so analyzed under headings and sub-headings as to be a book of reference. Systematic and detailed, its doctrine is classical in referring everything ultimately to ancient principles. Its exemplification is abundant, with the usual preference for Petrarch.

Book I, discussing epic, includes the *Divina Commedia* and Petrarch's *Trionfi,* and insists that the lack of unity in Ariosto's *Orlando* is a cardinal fault. If the teaching of the ancients "and the example of Homer's poetry is true, I do not see how another, different from that, is admissible; for truth is one. Therefore the variation of later times will not suffice as a warrant for letting a poem treat more than one action, entire and of just compass, to which everything else should be contributory" (35). What offends Minturno especially is Ariosto's interruption and resumption.

Book II, discussing drama, though it gives a better account of Aristotle's theory than the *De poeta,* still cites Horace, calls actors *recitanti,* and does not comprehend the idea of a play as a sequence of action.

Book III, dealing with lyric forms, is especially ample as to *canzone.* The triad of Pindar's odes he calls *volta, rivolta, stanza.* His own praises of Charles V consist of five such triads. "As Pindar," he goes on, "narrates the myths of Tantalus and Pelops, so I told the landing of Aeneas in Africa and Hannibal's invasion of Italy, with due reference to the Trojan origin of the Romans and of the princely ancestors of Charles" (183–184). After due citation of Dante the book goes on to *sonetto, ballata,* and other forms with both quotation and analysis, and even devotes a page to reminder of the Latin hymns.

Book IV analyzes style under the headings of the classical *elocutio* and *compositio,* and with detailed consideration of metric. The counsels for imitation, though tolerating the usual Renaissance closeness, stop short of Ciceronianism. The concluding advice for revision is drawn from Horace.

8. PARTENIO

Bernardino Partenio devoted five books to *Imitation in poetry (Della imitatione poetica . . .* Venice, 1560). A vernacular dialogue of the *De oratore* type, it achieves little interchange of views and interposes much delay by ceremonious introduction and interruption. At Murano, near Venice, the main speakers are two elders, Trifone and Trissino, and two younger, Paolo Manutio and Lunisini. The literary fiction is of instructing the latter; but whereas Lunisini remains most of the time silent, Manutio speaks often and sometimes at length. A few other persons pass across the background.

I. After the conventional introduction of poetry as the original philosophy, poetic composition is left to Aristotle and Horace, and poetic style is proposed (7) for discussion by a most confusing division: (1) *inventioni* through topics; (2) *assontioni,* which also should mean topics, but are further described as *commenti* and *fittione poetiche* (mythology); *ordine,* conceived as amplification and variation; (4) *affetti,* passions and moral habit; (5) *epiteti.*

Imitation (11–13) is common, natural, even necessary, in spite of objectors and of Pico's assertion that what we should follow is the *idea,* not the form. We may imitate a whole subject (17), or particular *sententiae,* or words, changing the order, amplifying or restricting, modifying. So did the ancients (24); so Bembo imitated Petrarch (25); and Terence defended his use of Menander (28). Camillo's topics (34) for poetical *inventio* are set forth with many examples. Partenio's application seems to amount to (1) mere periphrasis, (2) concrete specification, (3) amplification.

II. The next book makes plainer that imitation is dilation, especially in the direction of sophistic show-pieces (as in the use of Catullus, 73). The book is not really distinct from I. Perhaps that explains the padding (80 seq.) with discussion of poetic diction: compounds, polysyllables, figures. It closes with a survey of Sannazaro, Pontano, Fracastoro, Vida, Navagero, and the chief of vernacular poets, Bembo (86).

III. Imitation may mean the expression of human life; but specifically it is directed toward elegance of diction (93–95), and may involve the lifting of phrases (98). The awareness of style which comes from reading should be so confirmed by imitation (105) as to insure a poetic fund (*copia*). Imitation of style has always been legitimate (106), but with variations (110). Boccaccio's Ser Ciapeletto is dilated by a list of specifications (119), and concludes, as it should, with a *sententia.* But dilation demands also the use of topics (*assontioni*). These are exhibited in tabular view (123) and exemplified from Vergil, Horace, Catullus, and Petrarch.

IV. Further examples lead into mythology. Order of items in the encomium recipe may be varied (155). Imitation of passions is exemplified in Vergil's Turnus.

V. discusses appropriateness of style (*decoro*) under the seven *ideas* of Hermogenes (175), the nine *sensi,* and the eight instruments.

We have also learned earlier in this confusion that art not only comes from nature, but is a surer and more definite guide (35). Better take epithets from the ancient poets than hunt for them (162). Orators must use common speech; not so poets. Poetic diction should be not only appropriate and sonorous, but remote from daily speech (80).

Partenio's main significance is the propagation of Camillo's doctrine of topics derived from Hermogenes[5] and transferred to poetic. Thus it exhibits the common confusion both of poetic with rhetoric and of composing with writing a theme. Its abundant examples are misapplied to show how poetry may be brought on by dilation, which belongs not to poetry, but to oratory. The whole treatise might be called an art of dilation. It has hardly anything to do with writing poetry, almost everything to do with poetifying themes.

9. SCALIGER

Julius Caesar Scaliger achieved the longest Renaissance Latin poetic (*Julii Caesaris Scaligeri viri clarissimi poetices libri septem . . . 1561*).[6] Its complacency must have been sometimes startling even to the Renaissance. The prefatory letter to his son Sylvius is magisterial.

To this art we have applied the sanctions of philosophy, which are the executives of all nature. That for lack of them it has hardly been an art before us is evident from our discussion (iii).

Horace, though he has written an "ars poetica," teaches

---

[5] For Hermogenes, see MRP, pp. 23 ff.
[6] References are to the second edition of 1581. See also F. M. Padelford, *Select Translations from Scaliger's Poetics* (New York, 1905).

with so little art that almost the whole work seems nearer to satire. The commentaries of Aristotle, as we have them, are incomplete. The prudent Vida gives much good advice toward making a poet more wary, but takes him as already accomplished to lead him to perfection. We have led him by the right way through all paths to the very end (iv).

From time to time he inserts reminders of his magistracy.

Thus far Aristotle; but a more accurate account is as follows (46).
For thus, with more penetration than Aristotle's . . . (201).
No one before us has reduced figures to definite classification (307).
So much for *inventio*. With greatest toil amid many difficulties we have elaborated these precepts, which before us either were not explained at all, or, scattered without art or order, were merely implied, or were in substance or expression inept (432).
The Greeks are mistaken if they think we have taken anything from them except to improve it (598).
As if we were servants of the Greeklings, and not correctors (623).

His learning is too large to be limited to the subject. "Not to omit anything that makes for erudition" (170), he inserts, for example, a long chapter (I. xviii) on dancing, and another (III. ci) on Roman marriage customs. He is even from time to time autobiographical.

We too have labored not a little that this glory [of *hymnus* in its ancient sense] might be less obscure among the Latins (123).
We too celebrated our father, brave as he was unfortunate, in pastoral (129).
Under the title Senio we had written such a *fabula,* and

sustained the tone with Batavian chime and with such novelty of invention as might suffice for seven Erasmuses, to say nothing of one (374).

As we wrote in the epitaph of those who fell at Vienna in the war against the Turks (426).

His longest quotation (VI. 781–784) is an entire poem of his own.

The seven books of this vast poetic in 310 chapters and 944 pages are as follows.

I. *Historicus* (57 chapters, 136 pages) presents poetic forms: pastoral, comedy, tragedy, mime, *satira,* dance, Greek games, Roman festivals, lyric.

II. *Hyle* (*Materia,* 42 chapters, 64 pages) is mainly devoted to verse-forms.

III. *Idaea* (127 chapters, 238 pages) discusses under the sophistic topics (sex, occupation, moral habit, fortune, endowments, etc.) the *personae* of the poet's creation; sets forth the four poetic virtues (*prudentia, efficacia, varietas, figura*); and adds precepts for the several poetic forms.

IV. *Parasceve* (49 chapters, 98 pages) discusses the qualities of style, with additions on figures.

V. *Criticus* (17 chapters, 227 pages) is mainly a series of comparative parallels (*comparationes*), first by authors (Homer with Vergil, Vergil with Theocritus, etc.), then by topics (691–717).

VI. *Hypercriticus* (7 chapters, 134 pages) is a review of Latin poetry from the sixteenth century back.

VII. *Epinomis* (11 chapters, 47 pages) is an appendix.

Evidently the division overlaps; and the treatment involves even further repetition. For the book is not a consecutive treatise; it is rather a cyclopedia. Composed generally in short chapters, it indicates the subject of each

by a heading, and exhibits all the headings at the beginning in a full table of contents. Thus its vogue may have
been mainly for reference. Since it is a guide, not an
anthology, the examples are usually brief. Longest naturally in V, the book of parallels, they are elsewhere
sometimes only single lines, and rarely exceed ten. Though
the great exemplar is Vergil, who almost monopolizes
III and IV, they exhibit a wide range.

The object proposed is to form Latin poets: *poetam
creare instituimus* (200); *quoniam perfectum poetam
instituimus* (228). The book sets forth by precept and
example not only how to admire and criticize—and correct even famous authors, but how to attain the company
of Latin poets, how to make Latin poetry. The history of
Latin poetry includes the sixteenth century, though not
the Middle Age. Latin poetry has been recovered; and
Scaliger, as one of its poets and one of its critics, shows
how it is to be carried forward. Surveying it up and down
its length, he gives much space to Claudian, Statius, and
Silius Italicus, corrects Horace and Ovid, rewrites Lucan
(849), estimates his own immediate predecessors. He is
a schoolmaster giving *praelectiones* and correcting Latin
themes, extending his instruction by summoning to his
desk all authors and all times. He has read everything.
Careful to quote the Greeks abundantly in Greek, he as-
serts the superiority of the Latins. For one author only he
has nothing but admiration. His great exemplar, his
touchstone, is Vergil.

To pass from Scaliger's views on individual poets and
poetic methods to his view of poetic as a whole is not easy,

and is no longer important. As to imitation, his lack of specific precepts suggests that he has no consistent theory. The Aristotelian idea, apparently accepted at the beginning, is misinterpreted in the appendix. The usual Renaissance advice to imitate only with hope of adding luster, rhythm, or other charm (*lucem, numeros, venerem adiungere*, 700) refers, of course, to the other sort of imitation and offers little guidance. On the other hand, Scaliger laments his own early Ciceronianism (800), and makes some acute incidental observations. The topics of sophistic encomium in III, the stock comparisons in V. xiv, and occasional use of terms throughout show the usual Renaissance confusion of poetic with rhetoric. Though in other passages Scaliger seems able to conceive poetry in its own terms, he does not present poetic consistently as a distinct art of composition. Indeed, what he says about composition of either sort is often meager or formal. His preoccupation, from lexicography to figures of speech, is with style. The great apparatus for the production of Latin poetry remains largely rhetoric.

10. RONSARD AND TASSO

Ronsard's brief, hasty, and perfunctory *L'Art poétique* (1565; reprinted, with five prefaces, Cambridge University Press, 1930) shows the Pléiade preoccupation with "enriching" the vernacular,[7] and applies the sophistic recipe for encomium to the poet's celebration of great persons in odes.

[7] See above, Du Bellay, Chapter II, pp. 3, 6.

"The true aim of a lyric poet is to celebrate to the extreme him whom he undertakes to praise . . . his race . . . his native place" . . . (29). Enhancing his diction above common speech (41–44), he will amplify, even dilate.

The terms *invention* and *disposition,* transferred conventionally from rhetoric, do not open anything specific on composition.

Ronsard refers early to the relation of lyric to music. Except for a few such references, he has been content to gather commonplaces on style. The only importance of the treatise is in showing one of the foremost sixteenth-century poets driven, when asked for theory, as it were inevitably to rhetoric.

Tasso's poetic, on the other hand, is the most serious, concise, and penetrative of the Renaissance. Composed in 1568 and 1570 to be read before the Ferrara Academy, the *Discorsi dell'arte poetica ed in particolare sopra il poema eroico* were later amplified, in *Poema eroico* c. 1590 and *Discorsi dell'arte poetica,* 1587, for Tasso's theory was no less studious than his practice. Though he too uses the headings of rhetoric *inventio* and *dispositio,* he applies them to distinctively poetic conception and poetic movement. For he discusses poetic specifically and consistently as movement and as poetic movement. The inspiration is the *Poetic* of Aristotle. Working independently, Tasso grasped Aristotle's animating ideas at about the same time as Castelvetro in his illuminating commentary (1570).[8] The following references are to Solerti's edition of the *Discorsi* (1901).

[8] See H. B. Charlton, *Castelvetro's Theory of Poetry* (Manchester, 1913).

The epic poet should move in his own Christian faith and history, not among pagan deities and rites (12). His field must not be too large (23–25); his narrative scheme (*favola*), as Aristotle says, must be entire, of manageable scope, and single (28). For unity (33), in spite of critical disputes, in spite of Ariosto's success without it and of Trissino's failure with it, is vital. Ariosto prevails (46) not through lack of unity, but because of his excellence in other directions. Variety (47) is desirable only if it does not risk confusion; and, properly considered, it is compatible with unity. [A clear and just rebuttal; there is no value in variety unless there is something from which to vary.]

Part III (Style), opening with the rhetorical tradition of the "three styles," finds the third, *magnifico* (the Latin *grande*), appropriate to epic (52). [Tasso's own practice of *magnifico* is neither florid nor dilated.] Ariosto's style is *medium;* Trissino's, *tenue.* Tragedy (53), relying oftener on specific words (*proprio*), is less *magnifico;* lyric is more flowered and adorned; epic, though ranging between the two, is normally *magnifico.*

Adding (55–60) a summary of the rhetoric of style, including figures, Tasso finds Boccaccio's prose over-rhythmical. His appreciation of the force of exact words in Dante is refreshing after the earlier disparagement. He closes with an illuminating comparison (63) of epic style in Vergil with lyric in Petrarch.

Even contributions so distinctive as these are less important than the work as a whole. Tasso's treatise is so consecutive and so well knit as to be worth more than the sum of its parts. Alike in his order and in his sentences he is firmer and more severe than his time. These *Discorsi* are carefully planned and adjusted for teaching. They seek neither the conversational ease of Castiglione nor the seriatim analysis of Macchiavelli; and they are far removed from the discursive suggestions of Montaigne. They constitute a reasoned, consecutive poetic.

II. SIDNEY

Sidney's *Defense of Poesy* (about 1583; edited by Albert S. Cook, Boston, 1890) exhibits its moral function from mere moralizing, through winsome teaching, to incitement toward higher living.

The reminiscences of rhetoric are not accidental. Sidney makes the usual Renaissance transfer to poetry of the traditional threefold function of oratory: to teach, to delight, to move (9, 11, 13, 22, 26). Toward the end (55) he apologizes. "But what! methinks I deserve to be pounded [imprisoned] for straying from poetry to oratory. But both have such an affinity in the wordish consideration . . ." [i.e., in diction; but the main defect of the treatise is in leaving vague the distinctive character of poetic composition].

Moralizing, deviating to rhetoric, Sidney is nevertheless suggestive and sometimes penetrative.

He cites Plato's dialogues (3) as poetical. His lively account of poetry as imaginative realization (4–6) and as insight into human life makes clear Aristotle's saying that poetry "is more philosophical and more studiously serious than history" (18). He satirizes Elizabethan ignoring of the dramatic unities (48), and sees through Ciceronianism (53). His section (55–56) on the character and capacity of English verse, all too brief, has real importance.

But he is so far from grasping Aristotle's idea of imitation that he renders it thus:

Poesy, therefore, is an art of imitation, for so Aristotle termeth it in his word μίμησις, that is to say, a representing, counterfeiting, or figuring forth; to speak metaphorically, a speaking picture, with this end, to teach and delight (9).

We leap away from Aristotle to Horace's *ut pictura poesis,* and so to rhetoric. This is not merely misinterpretation; it indicates Sidney's lack of any controlling poetic principle. Though he tidily provides summaries at the ends of his sections, he has little advance of thought. His work is what it is called, a defense[9] of poetry, not a reasoned theory.

There is occasional significance in the usual Renaissance array of names. Paying his respects to the Cardinals Bembo and Bibbiena (44), Sidney immediately offsets them with the Protestants Beza and Melancthon. He calls Fracastoro and Scaliger "learned philosophers"; Pontano and Muret, "great orators"; and refers twice to the Latin tragedies of George Buchanan. His praise of l'Hospital (45) is probably reminiscent of Ronsard's ode; for Sidney is acquainted with the Pléiade. Boccaccio, Petrarch, and Ariosto he merely mentions; but he knows the greatness of Dante and of course the charm of Sannazaro. Of the ancients, Plato is cited oftenest, then Aristotle, Plutarch, Horace of course, and Pindar. He speaks of "the height of Seneca's style" (47), mentions Apuleius (50), and cites the "Greek Romances" in an extraordinary miscellany: "so true a lover as Theagenes, so constant a friend as Pylades, so valiant a man as Orlando, so right a prince as Xenophon's Cyrus, so excellent a man every way as Virgil's Aeneas" (8). His review of English poetry (45–47) scorns the intrusion of "base men with servile wits," finds that

---

[9] Lodge's feebler *Defence of Poetry* (1579) has little other interest than the historical, i.e., as a reply to Gosson's attack on the stage.

Chaucer "did excellently"—for his time, and gives vague praise to Surrey and Spenser. The reading of the English gentleman poet has been wide, creditably classical, undiscriminating.

12. ENGLISH DISCUSSION OF VERSE

George Gascoigne's *Certaine notes of instruction concerning the making of verse or rime in English,* written at the request of Master Edouardo Donati (1575; reprinted in G. Gregory Smith's *Elizabethan Critical Essays,* I, 46–57) is a brief primer of English verse usage. Though it bungles in detail, it is fairly true to the English tradition of rhythm determined by stress.

The last years of the century prolonged in England a proposal to classicize English metric. William Webbe's *Discourse of English Poetrie* (1586; Gregory Smith, I, 226–302. References are to these pages.) harps uncertainly on classical prosody.

What shoulde be the cause that our English speeche . . . hath neuer attained to anie sufficient ripeness, nay not ful auoided the reproch of barbarousness in poetry? (227) . . . What credite they might winne to theyr natiue speeche, what enormities they might wipe out of English Poetry . . . if English Poetrie were truely reformed (229).

A traditional preface on the origin of poetry leads from divine inspiration through early bards to Ovid moralized, Horace, and Mantuan (231–239). After dismissing medieval rhymed Latin as "this brutish poetrie," Webbe proceeds to a review of English achievement.

"I know no memorable worke written by any Poet in our English speeche vntill twenty yeeres past (239).

"Chawcer . . . was next after [Gower] . . . Though the manner of hys stile may seeme blunte and course to many fine English eares at these dayes, yet . . . a man shall perceiue . . . euen a true picture of perfect shape of a right poet. . . . Neere in time . . . was Lydgate . . . comparable with Chawcer (241). The next . . . Pierce Ploughman . . . somewhat harsh and obscure, but indeede a very pithy wryter . . . the first . . . that obserued the quantity of our verse without the curiosity of ryme" (242). A review of the sixteenth century surrounds Surrey and Sidney with an array of second-rate poets.

Taking a fresh start with the division into "comicall, tragicall, historiall," Webbe finds that Chaucer (251), even as Horace (250), mingled delight with profit. After a vague word for John Lyly (256) he returns to Golding's translation of Ovid (262). "Somewhat like, but yet not altogether so poetical" is Chaucer, whom he seems to have on his conscience. "But nowe yet at the last," and comparable with the best, is Spenser (263). A brief return to the ancients proceeds from Hesiod through Vergil to Tusser and Googe (265).

But Webbe still wishes that rhyme were not habitual. "Which rude kinde of verse . . . I may not vtterly dissalowe [266]. I am perswaded the regard of wryters to this hath beene the greatest decay of that good order of versifying which might ere this haue beene established in our speeche" (274). He even finds in English a "rule of position" (281), and that -ly is short in adverbs, long in adjectives (282). Stubbornly he closes his stupid book with an appendix (290): "Heere followe the Cannons or general cautions of poetry, prescribed by Horace, first gathered by Georgius Fabricius Chemnicensis."

Deaf to the tradition of English verse, Webbe is blind to the development of English poetry.

Puttenham's more pretentious *Arte of English Poesie* (1589; reprinted in part by G. Gregory Smith, II, 1–193), after the obligatory rehearsal of ancient seers, reads history thus.

"How the wilde and sauage people vsed a naturall poesie in versicle and rime as our vulgar is" (chapter v); and "How the riming poesie came first to the Grecians and Latins, and had altered and almost spilt their maner of poesie" (chapter vi). Classification into heroic, lyric, etc., and then into comedy, tragedy, ode, elegy, etc., is followed (chapter xxxi) by a review of English poetry as meager for a roll of honor as it is undiscriminating in criticism.

Book II, Proportion Poeticall, is a misguided prosody. "Proportion" is exhibited (chapter ii) in "staff" (i.e., stave or stanza); (iii) in "measure" (i.e., feet) estimated by the number of syllables without assigning a distinct function to "accent"; (v) in caesura ranged with "comma, colon, periodus," terms transferred from rhetoric to serve as aspects of rhythm; (vi and following) in "concord," which includes rime, accent, time, "stir," and "cadence"; (xi) in "position"; and finally in "figure," square stanzas, triangles, ovals, suitable to emblems and other devices. Through this confusion and deviation the typical English stress habit glimmers so faintly as never to be distinct. "How Greek and Latin feet might be applied in English" (xiii) leads in the closing chapters to "a more particular declaration of the metrical feet of the ancient poets."

Book III, Ornament, is a long and elaborate classification of figures of speech.[10] It ends conventionally with typical faults, with decorum, and, in tardy caution, with Horace's *ars celare artem.*

At the end of the sixteenth century, then, these English-

[10] In Smith's reprint shortened by summary.

men could still assume, with Ascham fifty years earlier, that English poetry had no valid tradition of its own, still seek to revive it by classicism. That classicism should be not only revival of ancient stanza and imitation of ancient style, as with the Pléiade, but even conformity to ancient metric might rather have been proposed in France or Italy, where vernacular verse had kept much of the Latin rhythmical habit. In England, where the vernacular tradition determined the verse pattern by the Germanic habit of stress, the proposal was foredoomed as futile. The insistence of the classical cult nevertheless lingers in serious discussion. The correspondence of Gabriel Harvey with Spenser on this point may be playful, or even partly satirical; but Harvey was a fanatic, and even Spenser sometimes read Chaucer's verse strangely, sometimes in his poetical youth made strange experiments. The item that lingered longest in discussion, perhaps because it was common to both verse traditions, is rhyme. Thomas Campion's *Arte of English Poesie* (1602)[11] attacked this specifically and with more understanding of English rhythms than Webbe had or Puttenham. Samuel Daniel replied with a correct but feeble *Defence of Ryme* (1603).[12] Classicism could attempt to deviate English verse the more easily when even poets and men of some learning did not understand the linguistic development of their own vernacular.

[11] Gregory Smith, II, 327–355.
[12] Gregory Smith, II, 356–384; Arthur Colby Sprague, *Samuel Daniel, Poems and a Defence of Ryme* (Cambridge, Harvard University Press, 1930).

13. PATRIZZI

Patrizzi's poetic (*Della poetica di Francesco Patrici la deca disputata* . . . Ferrara, 1586) renews the quarrel with Aristotle begun in his rhetoric.

The sub-title goes on: "in which by history, by arguments, and by authority of the great ancients is shown the falsity of the opinions most accepted in our times concerning poetic. There is added the *Trimerone* of the same author in reply to the objections raised by Signor Torquato Tasso[13] against his defence of Ariosto." The ten sections severally inquire: I concerning poetic inspiration (*furore poetico*), II whether poetry originated in the causes assigned by Aristotle, III whether poetry is imitation, IV whether the poet is an imitator, V whether poetry can be written in prose, VI whether plot (*favola*) is rather distinctive of the poet than verse, VII whether Empedocles as a poet was inferior to Homer, VIII whether poetry can be made from history, IX whether ancient poems imitated by harmony and rhythm, X whether the modes of imitation are three.

The divisions obviously overlap, and there is confusion in VII (152) between the origin of poetry and its essential character, in VIII (168) between historical material and history. Section VIII also misses the point of Aristotle's creative characterization for poetic consistency. These misinterpretations, common enough at the time, are due with Patrizzi to his missing Aristotle's idea of imitation as the distinctive poetic form of composition. Aristotle thinking of composition remains dark or wrong to Patrizzi thinking of style.[14] Thus he is typical of that

[13] Patrizzi's refutation of Tasso, 68, 116, 144/5, 173, 175.

[14] Nevertheless two of his references (V. 116; VI. 125) suggest, perhaps without his intention, a relation between Plato's *Symposium* and Aristotle's idea of creative imitation.

general Renaissance difficulty with Aristotle which came from looking the other way. Even after Tasso and Castelvetro, Renaissance poetic kept its preoccupation with style.

14. DENORES

Jason Denores, on the contrary, made his *Poetica* a digest of Aristotle with a tabular view at the end of each section (*Poetica di Iason Denores, nella qual per via di definitione & divisione si tratta secondo l'opinion d'Aristotele della tragedia, del poema heroico, & della comedia* . . . Padua, 1588). The book has no critical grasp.

Section I (Tragedy) classifies characterization by types (good rulers, bad rulers, etc.) and by the sophistic headings for encomium. "Appropriateness of the traits of the tragic personae consists in conformity (*decoro*) to age, emotion, sex, country, profession" (folio 24, verso). In a word, it is consistency. Chapter IX sums up what makes "una perfettissima tragedia"; and the concluding chapter (X) exemplifies an ideal tragic plot (*argomento*) by a novella of Boccaccio.

Section II (Epic) imposes the obligation of a single action as against the *Achilleis* of Statius, the *Metamorphoses* of Ovid, "and many of the romances of our time" (58). The *Aeneid* has not one action (63) and is not so well extended (*distesa*) as the *Odyssey* (66). Denores thinks that Aristotle intends the same demands as to plot (*favola,* Chapter I) and even as to component parts (Chapter VI) as for tragedy. Reviewing as before in Chapter IX, he again demonstrates in Chapter X by a story of Boccaccio.

Section III (Comedy) is merely an adaptation of the headings for tragedy. Denores even makes bold to say: "But since Aristotle seems to intend that the parts of comedy should be as many as for tragedy, therefore we have for convenience attributed to comedy prologue, episode, exode. The chorus we have not included, since in general it seems not to have been used" (folio 138, verso). This section, too, is concluded by a review and a demonstration from Boccaccio.

15.   VAUQUELIN

The poetic of the Sieur Vauquelin de la Fresnaye is important mainly for confirmation at the end of the century (*L'Art poétique de Vauquelin de la Fresnaye, ou l'on peut remarquer la perfection et le défaut des anciennes et des modernes poésies;* text of 1605 edited by Georges Pellissier,[15] Paris, 1885). Conceived in 1574 and embracing the ideas of the Pléiade, it was still unfinished in 1585 and finally published at Caen only two years before the gentleman poet's death. The latter part of the sub-title refers to the addition of a sort of *catalogue raisonné* of poets. Seventeen hundred and sixty Alexandrine couplets survey poetry in three books as style and metric; for composition enters rarely and in terms of rhetoric. Though Aristotle is cited, the base is once more the "Ars poetica" of Horace. Once more poetry is "speaking pictures" (I. 226); once more the Pléiade repudiates *balades* and *rondeaux* (I. 546). The doctrine of appropriateness (*bienséance, il decoro*) indicates characterization by type (II. 330; III. 499); and the ideal poetic combination is of instruction with delight (III. 609, *utile-dulce*). Instead of saying that Vauquelin outlived his age,[16] we may rather

---

[15] Pellissier's long introduction and valuable notes, though they need a few corrections by later studies, remain one of the most important surveys of the French development of poetic in the sixteenth century.

[16] But Vauquelin with Tasso bids poets leave pagan myth for Christian themes, though perhaps he refers only to subject; and he recognizes the place of Montemayor's *Diana* among pastorals.

reflect that change in doctrine had been slow and was not yet recognized generally.

16. SUMMARY

In the variety of these poetics appear certain habits and tendencies significant of the period. First, the Renaissance gentleman scholar finds it becoming not only to write verse, especially Latin verse, but to discuss poetic. Sound taste and informed judgment in poetry, as in painting and sculpture, give him rank as accomplished. The people assembled by Castiglione to discuss the ideal courtier agree on this; and indeed several of them might have written the dialogues examined above. Modern readers impatient at the willingness to talk from the book without independent thinking should beware of disparaging the value of a general obligation to be informed about poetry. But even the Renaissance gentlemen who were in the stricter sense scholars seem content with learning for itself. Instead of interpreting and advancing, they exhibit.

The confusion about imitation is too general to be attributed to the stupidity of individuals. It reflects the clash of two conceptions: Aristotle's idea of imitating human life [17] by focusing its actions and speech in such continuity as shall reveal its significance, an idea of composition; and the humanist idea of imitating classical style. As ideas, the two have nothing to do with each other; but they tripped each other in fact. For the first was new, not yet understood either exactly or generally; and the second was

[17] For Aristotle's *imitation*, see ARP, pages 139 ff.

a widespread habit of thought. Imitation suggested classicism. Aristotle, being an ancient, must in some way be
reconciled to this. Meantime it is evident, especially from
the more commonplace discussions, that though the theory
might not be clear, the practice inclined toward dilation
and borrowing. Ciceronianism, even while it waned, had
spread far beyond Cicero. Bembo's imitation of Petrarch
was not a reproach; it was an added virtue.

The cult of the great period does not preclude citation
of Claudian, Statius, Silius Italicus; and Scaliger adds
Ausonius and Sidonius. Even Apuleius is not excluded;
and space is occasionally found for the dullness of Aulus
Gellius and Macrobius. The "Greek Romances" of
Achilles Tatius, Apollonius or Heliodorus find place not
only with Cinthio, Scaliger, and Vauquelin, but also with
Ronsard and Sidney. Indeed, those poetic habits summed
up in the term Alexandrianism and corresponding to the
decadent rhetoric called sophistic, crop out often enough
to suggest a considerable vogue. The sophistic recipe for
encomium is accepted by Ronsard; and there is common
approval, in doctrine as in practice, of parenthetical dilation by descriptive show-pieces. So the rhetoric of Hermogenes, embraced by Camillo and Partenio for poetic,
is mentioned elsewhere with respect. Alexandrianism is at
least an inclination of the Renaissance.

But the commonest sign of the times is the unabated
vogue of Horace's "Ars poetica". It is gospel as much to
the Renaissance as it had been to the Middle Age. The
cynical explanation would be its very shallowness and
conventionality; but probably the deeper reason is that

Renaissance thinking on poetic, as Horace's, was essentially rhetorical. Here, at any rate, is the main significance of these poetics. Various as they may be otherwise, they have this in common. Tasso stands out as an exception, in theory as in practice, by his clear view of poetic as a distinct art of composition; and he is supported by Castelvetro's penetrative interpretation of the *Poetic* of Aristotle. But Vauquelin has not heard them; and even Sidney, though he sees the distinction, still falls back on rhetoric. Even to the end of the sixteenth century, Renaissance poetic was largely rhetoric.[18]

[18] D. L. Clark, *Rhetoric and Poetry in the Renaissance* (New York, 1922).

Chapter VIII

PROSE NARRATIVE

I. TALES

NOTHING is more characteristic of the Renaissance than the abundance of tales. Printed in large collections, they evidently answered a steady demand; and they furnished many plots for the Elizabethan stage. Often significant of Renaissance taste in stories, they are generally less interesting in narrative art.

(*a*) *Bandello*

Bandello dedicates each of his 224 *novelle* to some friend in a prefatory letter which usually represents it as actually told in his hearing by a person whom he names (*Le quattro parti de le novelle del Bandello riprodotte sulle antiche stampe di Lucca* [1554] *e di Lione* [1573] *a cura di Gustavo Balsamo-Crivelli,* Turin, 1910). The stories are further documented by proper names; or Bandello tells us that he has substituted fictitious ones to shield well-known families. *Novella* 16, for instance, of Part I "happened last winter in this city of Mantua." Though this and many others are conventional *fabliaux* or stock friar tales, they are all alike told for their news value, as striking or exciting. Bandello seems more intent on finding good stories than on making stories good. Hence he is more significant of the appetite and taste of his time than as a story-teller.

The Elizabethans, who often hunted in his collection, often through French or English translations, created from some of his persons characters as convincing as Juliet and the Duchess of Malfi; but characterization rarely detains Bandello himself. Since he may be content with a mere clever retort or a dirty trick, many of his tales are brief, and many of these are mere anecdote. Even so the obligatory introduction summarizing the situation may occupy a fourth, or even a third; and the rehearsal of the facts may suffice without the salience that would give them narrative interpretation.

Novella 9 of Part I in ten pages exhibits a husband so jealous as to violate the confessional and thereupon murder his wife. First displaying the luxury of Milan, the scene of the story, and even pausing to comment on the Milanese dialect, it proceeds to slow exposition of the situation, with dialogue of minor persons not active in the story, and with lingering over minor details. The only scene developed before our eyes is the violated confession. Thus bungled, the ugly story becomes more tedious than tragic.

Lack of salience, though not often so flagrant, is habitual. Without salience, without sufficient motivation, Bandello's tales are oftener a mere series of events than a sequence of scenes. They are not consistently developed by action. Instead of revealing themselves progressively before our eyes, his persons make speeches or even think aloud. Their speeches are far oftener oratory than narrative dialogue. Indeed, they may repeat what has been already thought or done. The very inequality in the collection betrays Bandello's weakness in narrative composition. His ornate style is fairly constant in elegant fluency;

but his composition is hit or miss. He has no steady command of story management.

Nor is his art sure in the eighteen longer tales. Of these, twelve (Part I. 5, 17, 21, 34, 45, 49; Part II. 24, 28, 36, 40, 41, 44), averaging about twenty-three pages, have essentially the same slack composition as the shorter tales. The remaining six deserve more attention.

I. 2 (26 pages) Ariobarzanes, proud and generous courtier, endured from Artaxerxes a series of humiliations, and emerged triumphant. The tale begins with the posing of a question: is the life of a courtier essentially liberality and courtesy, or obligation and debt? The series of trials is cumulative enough to give a certain sequence; but that it involved a struggle against detraction is not disclosed until the final oration, and thus does not operate as motivation.

I. 15 (23 pages) Two clever wives conspired to outwit the intrigues of their husbands, delivered them from prison, and reconciled them to each other. Here are complication and solution, but through a plot as artificial as it is ingenious. Though the detail is livelier, the action is slow. It halts in the middle; and the dénoument comes finally through a long oration rehearsing the whole story in court. The only characterization is of a third lady in the sub-plot.

I. 22 (25 pages) Timbreo, betrothed to Fenicia, repudiated her through a dastardly trick of his rival. The lady, who was supposed to be dead of shame, hid herself in a villa. The rival repenting and confessing, both men vowed to set her name right. At the request of her father marrying "Lucilla," Timbreo found her to be Fenicia. The rival married a sister, and the King adorned the wedding with royal festivities, dowries for the brides, and posts for the men. Here again are complication and solution. Though some of the scenes are realized, there is not that salience of critical situations which leads a narrative sequence onward. The royal wedding at the end, for instance, has as much space as the repudiation. Fenicia is presented with some hints of characterization.

I. 27 (27 pages) Don Diego and Ginevra, two very young country gentlefolk, falling in love utterly at sight, the girl turned so violently jealous as to deny all attempts at reconciliation; and the boy in despair went far away to end his days as a hermit in a cave. An old friend of both families, finding his retreat, reasoned with him in vain, but roused his hope by promising to move the girl. The girl was so far from being moved that she planned to elope with an adventurer. The old friend frustrated this and, in spite of the girl's fury, carried her off toward the boy's cave. Her pride remaining quite obstinate, the old friend finally lost patience and told her to go her own foolish way; but the boy, coming to meet them, showed so deep and unselfish devotion that she fell on his neck. This tale, which Bandello had from Spain, has not only complication and solution, but, in spite of some unnecessary interruption, an engaging narrative progress. Besides the constant motivation of the persons' youth, there is definite characterization of the old friend, of the boy, and especially of the girl. No other tale of the collection equals this in narrative composition.

II. 9 (35 pages) The now familiar tale of Romeo and Juliet is told straight through with little salience and with little characterization.

II. 37 (48 pages) Edward III, suing a lady long in vain, at last had to marry her. The lady's first high-spirited and intelligent response has some distinct characterization; but the situation is repeated again and again with cumulative urgency until this longest of the tales becomes tedious.

Even these better longer tales, then, are quite unequal in story management. Bandello seems to take his stories as he finds them. His literary fiction of writing a story that he has heard seems essentially true in that sense. As he has not discerned in Boccaccio the various achievement of a narrative artist, so he does not see what makes his own best tales good, much less shape others accordingly. He is not creative.

(b) Marguerite de Navarre

The collection of tales made by Marguerite de Navarre, probably with her literary household, and now known as the *Heptameron,* was first printed as *Les Amants fortunés* in 1558. Obviously patterned on Boccaccio's *Decameron,* it uses the literary frame of an aristocratic house party more realistically. The dialogue in comment on the stories is developed to characterize each person. Thus the collection is made a series of cases (*exempla*) for social comment. But the tales themselves are inferior. Told simply, without much flavor, "for fear" says the preface, "that beauty of style might prejudice historical truth," they are usually lucid, somewhat conversational, often lax. There is no mastery of narrative movement. The steadfast purity of the wife is, indeed, a constant motivation in II. 3; but the few salient scenes hardly constitute a sequence. The mere series of events in III. 1 makes eighteen pages tedious and ends in mere reversal. The dialogue of the retold *Châtelaine de Vergi* (VII. 10; 20 pages) is oftener oratory than narrative. The longest of the tales (I. 10; 32 pages), a romance covering years, has so little salience that it might as well have ended earlier. Most of the tales are either anecdote or *fabliau* of about seven pages. Put forward as actual, they are sometimes stock medieval tales, especially of the stupidity or brutality of friars, and where they appear to narrate facts, sometimes merely report them without realizing any moment as a scene. Boccaccio, too, has simple anecdotes, in which all the charm is of style; he too prolongs some of his stories without salience; but among his many experiments are five *novelle* (I. 4, II. 1 and 2, VIII. 8, IX. 6) intensified by their sequence. Far from noticing this difference, the writers of the *Heptameron* show little awareness of narrative composition. The accompaniment of discussion is better managed than the stories themselves.

(c) *Giraldi Cinthio*

The collection *Hecatommithi* (hundred fables) of Giovan-Battista Giraldi, known as Giraldi Cinthio,[1] accumulated through years. Begun apparently in his young manhood, it had reached seventy tales in 1560,[2] was published in 1565, and reprinted in 1566, 1574, 1580, and 1584.[3] (*Hecatommithi, ouero cento nouelle, di M. Giovanbattista Giraldi Cinthio,* nobile ferrarese: nelle quali, oltre le diletteuole materie, si conoscano moralità vtilissime a gli huomini per il benviuere, & per destare altresi l'intelletto alla sagacità; potendosi da esse con facilità apprendere il vero modo di scriuere toscano . . . 4th edition, Venice, 1580.) Thus the moralizing suggestion

---

[1] Cf. in Chapter VII Giraldi's theory of the romance.

[2] This is inferred from a commendatory letter of Bartolomeo Cavalcanti prefixed to this fourth (1580) edition.

[3] For editions and translations, see Louis Berthé de Besaucèle, *J.-B. Giraldi* (thesis at the University of Aix-en-Provence, Paris, 1920), pp. 109, 255, 258; for the French translator, Gabriel Chappuys, see p. 261.

of the title is confirmed by the sub-title. Here are offered one hundred—indeed, with the preliminary decade, one hundred and ten—*exempla*. Nor is the collection made less formidable by being classified: ten tales to exhibit the superiority of wedded love, ten to show the risks of dealing with courtesans, ten on infidelity, ten on chivalry, etc. Nevertheless the tales are not all moralities, and in some the moral is not even clear; for here once more are both *fabliaux* and anecdotes. The frame is once more Boccaccio's. Young aristocrats, escaped from the sack of Rome (1527), board ship and on a slow cruise entertain one another with tales. The style, though sometimes slack and diffuse, is not dilated for decoration. There is a leisurely introduction; each tale is prefaced by comment on the preceding; and each decade has an epilogue of discussion and verse. The whole ends with a roll of fame commemorating some hundred and fifty men of letters in *terza rima,* and adding a list of eminent ladies.

Running generally from three pages to ten, the tales, even the few that run to fourteen, remain scenario. II. ii. recounts in fourteen pages a Persian tale of Oronte and Orbecche. V. x. tells at the same length how the virtuous wife of Filogamo, shipwrecked, resisted the Prince of Satalia, and that he was thereupon expelled. In X. viii two quarreling nobles come to blows, are imprisoned by King Louis, and subsequently reconciled by the courtesy of one. Even the tale of the Moorish captain, which has hardly more than eight pages, is not developed narratively. Looking back to it from *Othello,* one distinguishes the motivation discerned by Shakspere; but in Giraldi's tale this is either generalized or merely hinted; it does not conduct the narrative.

The composition, then, is generally scenario. If the dialogue sometimes rises to narrative economy, it also becomes sometimes mere oration. Character, often merely typical, rarely suffices for motivation. Unnecessary spreading of the time-lapse betrays a carelessness of focus. There is no habit either of realizing scenes concretely in action, or of conducting them in a sequence.

A typical example is I. v. Pisti, condemned in, Venice for killing a man that had sought to debauch his wife, escaped to Ferrara and was banned. The situation is first propounded, and then recounted by his wife. She and his daughter being left in poverty, he wrote anxiously, urging them to maintain their honor. He was betrayed into captivity by two supposed friends, that their father, who was also under Venice ban, might by delivering him up reinstate himself. The father, refusing to take advantage of their treachery, liberated Pisti on condition that he forgive them. Pisti, returning secretly to Venice, bade his wife denounce him to the Signory and claim the reward for his head. She refused in an oration so fervent as to attract the guard, who thereupon arrested him. Going with him to court, she so told the whole story that the Signory pardoned Pisti, restored his property, gave the reward to his daughter for dowry, and even pardoned his false friends' father. The motivation of an ingenious complication and solution is all here—in the abstract. But the tale in eight pages merely sums up or orates instead of realizing it in scenes. The *novella* thus remains an *exemplum* of generosity, instead of becoming a story of Pisti's wife.

Thus Giraldi, seeking with Bandello news interest and therefore melodrama, proposing an edification often quite dubious, ignored the deeper narrative values. Reporter, manipulator, moralizer, he is not a creator.

(d) Belleforest, Painter, and Fenton

The collections of tales, then, show Renaissance story-telling as a regression from the fourteenth century. The narrative art of Boccaccio, to say nothing of Chaucer, has suffered eclipse. Far from being advanced, it is not even discerned. Renaissance story-telling is generally as inferior as it is abundant. The few well managed stories stand out in sharp relief against the mass of convention and of bungling. But this is not all. Bandello's tales as rendered (1566–1576) in French by Belleforest and in English through him by Painter and Fenton, are not merely translated; they are dilated and decorated to the point of being actually obscured as stories. Bandello's forty-ninth tale, already doubled by Belleforest, is trebled in Fenton's first. Livio and Camilla, told by Bandello in 1,500 words, has nearly 11,000 in Belleforest's twenty-second, and 16,731 in Fenton's second. The dilation is by show-pieces of description, by oratory, by moralizing, by allusions to classical mythology and to the "natural" history derived from Pliny, and by those balanced iterations known generically in English as euphuism. Belleforest in his preface (1568) begs the reader's pardon for not "subjecting" himself to the style of Bandello. "I have made a point," he says, "of recasting it." His *Continuation* informs the Duc d'Orléans in a dedication that he has "enriched with maxims, stories, harangues, and epistles." So Painter must pause to describe.

There might be seene also a certain sharpe and rude situation of craggy and vnfruictful rocks, which notwithstanding yelded some pleasure to the Eyes to see theym tapissed with a pale moasie greene, which disposed into a frizeled guise made the place pleasaunt and the rock soft according to the fashion of a couerture. There was also a very fayre and wide Caue, which liked him well, compassed round about with Firre trees, Pine apples, Cipres, and Trees distilling a certayne Rosen or Gumme, towards the bottom whereof, in the way downe to the valley, a man might haue viewed a passing company of Ewe trees, Poplers of all sortes, and Maple trees, the Leaues whereof fell into a Lake or Pond, which came by certaune smal gutters into a fresh and very cleare fountayne right agaynst that Caue. The knight viewing the auncientry and excellency of the place, deliberated by and by to plant there the siege of his abode for performing of his penaunce and life (Vol. III, p. 222, of the 1890 reprint).

Description for itself, without function, and even more plainly the other habitual means of decoration, show not only the general habit of dilation, but also the general carelessness of narrative values. So is smothered even the Spanish tale of Don Diego and Ginevra,[4] which Bandello had the wit, or the luck, to repeat in its original sequence. Evidently these versions were looking not to composition, not to the conduct of the story, but only to style.

(e) Pettie, Lyly, and Greene

William Pettie's *A Petite Pallace of Pettie His Pleasure, containing many pretie histories by him set forth in comely colours and most delightfully discoursed* (1576) iterates the medieval balance figures and reënforces them with alliteration. Thus his rendering of the tale of Scylla and Minos, after an expository summary and due moralizing, presents:

[4] See above, p. 198.

one Nisus, who had to daughter a damsel named Scilla, a proper sweet wench, in goodliness a goddess, in shape Venus herself, in shew a saint, in perfection of person peerless, but in deeds a dainty dame, in manners a merciless maid, and in works a wilful wench . . . But to paint her out more plainly, she was more coy than comely, more fine than well-favoured, more lofty than lovely, more proud than proper, more precise than pure.

If there be any place for such style, surely it is not in story. The story is hardly told; it is decorated, moralized, generalized without narrative salience. The decoration thus abused by Pettie became a vogue through John Lyly (1553?–1606). His *Euphues, the Anatomy of Wit* (1578) and *Euphues and His England* (1580) made the *schemata* of sophistic, especially isocolon, parison, and paromoion,[5] a main item in the curious style called euphuism.

Come therefore to me, all ye lovers that have been deceived by fancy, the glass of pestilence, or deluded by women, the gate to perdition; be as earnest to seek a medicine as you were eager to run into a mischief. The earth bringeth forth as well endive to delight the people as hemlock to endanger the patient, as well the rose to distil as the nettle to sting, as well the bee to give honey as the spider to yield poison (Croll's ed., p. 93).

Yet if thou be so weak, being bewitched with their wiles, that thou hast neither will to eschew nor wit to avoid their company, if thou be either so wicked that thou wilt not or so wedded that thou canst not abstain from their glances, yet at the least dissemble thy grief. If thou be as hot as the

[5] For the Gorgian figures, see MRP and Croll's introduction to his edition of *Euphues.*

mount Aetna, feign thyself as cold as the hill Caucasus, carry two faces in one hood, cover thy flaming fancy with feigned ashes, show thyself sound when thou art rotten, let thy hue be merry when thy heart is melancholy, bear a pleasant countenance with pined conscience, a painted sheath with leaden dagger (Ibid., p. 104).

The tiresome heaping of balances and allusions so cumbers narrative that these books keep little semblance of story.

Nevertheless the habit was continued in the longer English tales, sometimes called novels, of the 1580's and 90's. Greene's *Carde of Fancie* (1584–1587) decorates emotion with allusion and supplies balances by handfuls.

He manfullie marcht on towards her, and was as hastilie incountred by Castania, who embracing Gwydonius in her armes, welcommed him with this salutation.

As the whale, Gwydonius, maketh alwaies signe of great joye at the sight of the fishe called *Talpa Marina,* as the Hinde greatlie delighteth to see the Leopard, as the Lion fawneth at the view of the Unicorne, and as he which drinketh of the Fountaine Hipenis in Scithia feeleth his mind so drowned in delight that no griefe, though never so great, is able to assuage it, so, Gwydonius, I conceive such surpassing pleasure in thy presence, and such heavenlie felicitie in the sight of thy perfection, that no miserie though never so monstrous, is able to amaze me, no dolour though never so direfull is able to daunt me, nor no mishap though never so perillous is able to make me sinke in sorrow, as long as I injoy thy presence, which I count a soveraine preservative against all carefull calamities.

It is not necessary to regard this as quite serious to see that balanced iteration and learned allusion had become epidemic, and that both arise from the habit of dilation.

For even plain Thomas Deloney must decorate his clothier Jack of Newbury (1597) with myth and marvel. That such perversion of narrative, owing something now and then, perhaps, to the *Hypnerotomachia* or to Apuleius, is imitated more specifically from the Greek Romances is plainest in Sidney's *Arcadia*.[6] It is one of the clearest instances of Renaissance Alexandrianism.

2. RABELAIS

Émile Egger was once moved to protest: "The actual French usage of 1530 shows nowhere in either speech or writing the diction of Rabelais."[7] Every student of Rabelais will recognize this observation as a lead. It means much more than the truisms that every eminent author has his own style, and that study of style is the most constantly fruitful study of literature. It means that Rabelais makes the special demand of compelling attention always to his style. His vocabulary[8] ranges from Latinizing to dialect and jargon; his wordplay from reckless puns to various iteration; his cadences from the clausula of Cicero to mere lists. His volubility flashes with picturesque concreteness. He is popular, yes, but rarely in being simple, usually in talking with his readers and in stimulating them by extravagance. The fifteenth-century extravagance of Skelton, showing a similar volubility, has less display. Rabelais will not let us ever forget his style.

[6] Samuel Lee Wolff, *The Greek Romances in Elizabethan Prose Fiction* (New York, Columbia University Press, 1912).

[7] *Op. cit.*, pp. 173 seq. The quotation is at p. 177.

[8] H. Brown, *Rabelais in English Literature* (Harvard Press, 1933), p. 19.

Pantagruel rencontra un escolier tout joliet. . . "Mon amy, dond viens tu à ceste heure?" L'escolier luy respondit: "De l'alme, inclyte, et celebre academie que l'on vocite Lutece." "Q'est ce à dire?" dist Pantagruel à un de ses gens. "C'est," respondit il, "de Paris." "Tu viens donc de Paris," dit il. "Et à quoy passez vous le temps, vous autres estudians audit Paris?" Respondit l'escolier: "Nous transfretons la Sequane au dilucule et crepuscule, nous deambulons par les compites et quadrivies de l'urbe, nous despumons la verbocination latiale, et comme verisimiles amorabonds captons la benevolence de l'omnijuge, omniforme, et omnigene sexe feminin. . . . Et si par forte fortune y a rarité ou penurie de pecune en nos marsupies, et soient exhaustes de metal ferruginé, pour l'escot nous dimittons nos codices et vestes oppigncrées, prestolans les tabellaires à venirdes penates et lares patriotiques." A quoy Pantagruel dist "Quel diable de langage est cecy? Par dieu, tu es quelque heretique." "Segnor no," dist l'escolier; "car libentissimement des ce qu'illucesce quelque minutule lesche de jour, je demigre en quelqu'un de ces tant bien architectés monstiers, et là, me irrorant de belle eau lustrale, grignotte d'un transon de quelque missique precation de nos sacrificules. Et submirmillant mes precules horaires, elue et absterge mon anime de ses inquinamens nocturnes. Je revere les olympicoles. Je venere latrialement le supernel astripotens." Je dilige et redame mes proximes. Je serve les prescrits decalogiques, et selon la facultatule de mes vires n'en discede le late unguicule. . . . "Et bren, bren," dist Pantagruel, "Qu'est ce que veult dire ce fol? Je croy qu'il nous forge icy quelque langage diabolique, et qu'il nous charme comme enchanteur." A quoy dist un de ces gens: "Seigneur, sans nul doubte ce gallant veult contrefaire la langue des Parisiens; mais il ne fait que escorcher le latin, et cuide ainsi pindariser; et luy semble bien qu'il est quelque grand orateur en françois parce qu'il dedaigne l'usance commun de parler." A quoy dist Pantagruel, "Est il vray?" L'escolier respondit: "Segnor missayre, mon genie n'est point apte nate à ce que dit ce flagitiose nebulon, pour escorier la cuticule de nostre vernacule gallique; mais vice-versement je gnave, opere, et par veles et rames je me enite de le locupleter de la redondance latinicome." "Par dieu," dit Pantagruel, "je vous apprendray à parler" (II. vi).

The parody is of that Latinizing "enrichment" of the vernacular which was a wide preoccupation and the special creed of the Pléiade. Rabelais, as Erasmus, ridicules its paganizing. The larger satire is the rendering of the conventions of student wildness in an iterative learned jargon. For the iteration is not careless. Thus he prolongs a mere play upon the word *Sorbonne:*

. . . ces marauds de sophistes, sorbillans, sorbonagres, sorbinigenes, sorbonicoles, sorboniformes, sorbonisecques, niborcisans (II. xviii).

Thus he prolongs a parody of legal citations.

Ayant bien veu, reveu, leu, releu, paperassé, et feuilleté les complainctes, adjournemens, comparitions, commissions, informations, avant procedés, productions, allegations, intenditz, contredits, requestes, enquestes, repliques, dupliques, tripliques, escritures, reproches, griefz, salvations, recollements, confrontations, acarations, libelles, apostoles, lettres royaulx, compulsoires, declinatoires, anticipatoires, evocations, envoyz, renvoyz, conclusions, fins de non proceder, apoinctemens, reliefz, confessions, exploictz, et autres telles dragées et espiceries d'une part et d'autre, comme doibt faire le bon juge selon ce qu'en a *not. spec. de ordinario* § 3 *et tit. de offic. omn. jud.* § *fin. et de rescript. praesentat.,* § 1 (III. xxxix).

Thus the resolution of Diogenes to do his part in the defense of Corinth lets Rabelais stop to amplify the commonplaces of a siege.

When Philip threatened siege, the Corinthians prepared for defense. Some from the fields to the fortresses brought household goods, cattle, wine, food, and necessary munitions. Others repaired walls, raised bastions . . . [and so through a series of 25 predicates]. Some polished corselets [and so through another catalogue of particulars]. Diogenes girt his loins, rolled up his sleeves, gave his manuscripts to the charge of an old friend [and so through another series of details] . . . "Icy beuvant je delibere, je discours, je resouldz et concluds. Aprés l'epilogue je ris, j'escris, je compose, je boy. Ennius beuvant escrivoit, escrivant beuvoit. Eschylus (si à Plutarche foy avez in *Symposiacis*) beuvoit composant, beauvant composait. Homere jamais n'escrivit à jeun. Caton jamais n'escrivit qu'aprés boire." Thus the resolution gives occasion for eight pages. (Prologue to Tiers Livre.) As here, the amplification is often oratorical.

This various diffuseness, parody of Latinizing, legal iteration, oratorical amplitude, is gift of gab, oral expansiveness, passion for words; it is satire; and ultimately it is search for a reading public. Taking his cue from the almanacs and giant stories, Rabelais was exploiting the grotesque. He was clever enough to see that he could amuse not only the *bon bourgeois* who bought almanacs, but also those who had some pretensions to studies. Both, as Ariosto knew, found relaxation in the grotesque. The latter would appreciate technical jargon more; but the former would catch enough of its satire and get some amusement from its very strangeness. Both he could feed also with the marvels of voyages. For the grotesque is an adult fairyland.

Rabelais takes us in and out of it, back and forth. Though the work is largely narrative, it is not progressive

story. The persons, often vividly realized at a given moment, are not advancing to a destined issue. There is much
description, much discussion; and each has its effect rather
by itself than in a reasoned sequence. Thus the disgusting
story of the lady haunted by dogs, one of the most notorious of his incidental *nouvelles,* is told quite as much for
its own shock as for any turn it gives to the larger story.

On the whole, Rabelais' writing is *conte,* though usually involving some exposition in aim and some actual comment. The series of *exempla* and opinions as to whether
Panurge shall marry (III. xxi, seq.) reaches neither
a decision on the marriage nor a conclusion of character.
We find ourselves discussing the mendicant friars, listening to a discourse on devils, and ending on sheer lore
about the herb Pantagruelion (III. xlix, seq.). All the
while the concreteness of the rendering is vivid in contrast
to the conventional generalities of the collections of tales.
The dialogue, instead of being exchange of orations,
sometimes flashes with narrative interaction. Rabelais takes
us traveling, as it were, through many excitements with
a group of voluble grotesques whose ideas are not developed in sequences of paragraphs, nor their habits in
sequences of chapters. He opened both novel and essay
without achieving the form of either. For he was moving
toward that other kind of story and discussion which
ripened in journalism. Integration and continuity are less
important to attract readers than abundance and animation. Instead of making a point, he often hovers around
it with many suggestions. Instead of giving a scene distinct significance to lead into the next, he plays it with

many overtones. Unsystematic as his various abundance is certainly, and sometimes confusing, it must be recognized as creative. Rabelais is not content merely to rehearse, paraphrase, or decorate. Charged with various lore, his work is never second-hand. What he seizes he animates.

The satire of Rabelais, as distinct from his more descriptive ridicule, is directed oftenest against pedantry. The idea that he satirizes the Middle Age as an apostle of Renaissance enlightenment extends a dubious contrast beyond the evidence. For Rabelais is in some aspects medieval. He was a wandering scholar, a *vagans;* he was something of a *goliard;* and in the way of Godescalc he was a *mauvais clerc.* His satire on monks and friars is medieval literary stock. Indeed, it is much less attack, still less reform, than excitement. Against medieval education he does not urge Renaissance enlightenment except in irony.

In a letter of June 3, 1532, he raised a disconcerting question.

How comes it, most learned Tiraqueau, that in the abundant light of our century, in which by some special gift of the gods we see all the better disciplines recovered, there are still found everywhere men so constituted as to be either unwilling or unable to lift their eyes from the more than Cimmerian darkness of the gothic time to the evident torch of the sun?[9]

The irony of this is iterated and underlined in the oft-quoted eighth chapter of his *Pantagruel,* where Gargantua recalls his youth.

[9] *Cf.* Budé, Chapter I, for Renaissance complacency.

As you may easily understand, the times were not so suited, so convenient for literature, as the present, and had few such teachers as you have had. The times were still dark, and still exhaled the awkwardness and ill luck of the Goths, who had destroyed all good literature. But by divine goodness light and dignity have been restored to literature in my time; and I see such improvement that at present I should hardly be received in the beginning class, though as a man I used to be reputed the most learned of my time. I say this not in vain boasting, though I might legitimately do so in writing to you (see Marcus Tullius *De senectute* and Plutarch in the book entitled *How to praise oneself without reproach*), but to show you my deep affection.

Nowadays all the disciplines have been restored, the languages reëstablished: Greek, without which 'tis a shame for any one to call himself learned, Hebrew, Chaldee, Latin; printed editions as elegant as correct in usage, which were invented in my time by divine inspiration, as artillery by suggestion of the devil. The whole world is full of scholars, of most learned teachers, most ample libraries; and it seems to me that neither the time of Plato nor that of Cicero offered such convenience for study as is seen now. Hereafter we need not find in office or in society any one unpolished by the shop of Minerva. I see brigands, executioners, adventurers, stableboys of today more learned than the doctors and preachers of my time. Nay more, women and girls have aspired to that praise and celestial manna of good instruction.

What is pierced here is not medieval ignorance, but Renaissance complacency. The pedantry that Rabelais satirizes is of both ages. His quarrel with the Sorbonne of his own day may have been edged by the banning of *Pantagruel*. The book was banned as obscene. It is obscene. Let us no longer pretend that he attacked obscurantism as a champion of enlightenment. For whatever his motive, Rabelais remained singularly detached. He was far from being an apostle of enlightenment, or of anything else.

Yet he is still cited in some histories as forecasting modern education. An educational theory has been extracted from him, even a scheme. To support this, his conventional or picturesque ridicule of university teaching and of student manners is at most negative. A positive contribution has been found in his abbey of Thelème (I. lii–lviii).

Thelème, the ideal abbey that is the scene of the so-called scheme of education, takes its name probably from that preposterous allegory *Hypnerotomachia*,[10] wherein the hero forsakes the guidance of Reason (Logistica) for that of will (Thelemia). Its architecture and landscape gardening, again reminding of Colonna's pseudo-classical elaboration, receive, with the furniture and accessories, ten times as much space as the studies. It has 9,332 suites. Its library abounds in Greek, Latin, Hebrew, French, Tuscan, and Spanish (omitting English and German); and its frescoes are of "antiques prouesses." Outside are fountains, a hippodrome, a theater, swimming pool, garden, labyrinth, tennis court, and park. Inside it is supplied with costumers and furnishers. Its community of men and women, all handsome, richly dressed, and commanding the six languages well enough to compose in prose and verse, has no community obligation. Living in luxury, with the six languages among their pastimes, freed from

[10] Above, Chapter II.

the world and from all duties to one another, these priv-
ileged souls have for their community device "Fais ce
que voudras."

The humor of this, which ought to be discernible even
to those preoccupied with schemes of education, might
more easily be taken to imply that irresponsibility plus
command of languages is not a sufficient educational formula even in an ideally luxurious environment. Since this
would be a shrewd satire on the Renaissance, it may well
be what Rabelais meant. Certainly he did not mean to
propose Thelème for adoption as an idea, much less as a
scheme. Do as you please, provided you live in luxury
and command six languages. Is that an educational idea?
Is it by any tenable interpretation an educational scheme?
To range Rabelais with such pioneers of the fifteenth century as Guarino and Vittorino, or with such coming leaders as Vives and Loyola, is not only to misinterpret him;
it is to do him wrong. His satire is not limited to the loud
and boisterous; he is master also of irony. Let Thelème
rest as he left it, an ironical fantasy.

Nor should Gargantua's studious day (I. xxiii), no hour
unfilled, no subject neglected, be called a program of
education.[11] Rabelais must have been aware that for educational reform he had no warrant. Whatever else may be
laid to his charge, he was not pretentious. His own education, interrupted, never carried through in any field, but
widely ranging, gave him not a system, but a singularly
various fund. His reputation for scholarship, recently
urged, is hardly borne out by the few contemporary com-

[11] J. Plattard, *François Rabelais* (Paris, 1932), p. 194.

pliments. Rather their fewness and their vagueness, in a period of mutual admiration among scholars, suggest that he was less famous than he has been made to appear. He was not Latinist enough to detect the fabrication of the so-called *Will of Lucius Cuspidius,* which he published in 1532.[12] His Greek, extending to the translation of certain well-known Greek works of medicine,[13] may have been fortified by previous Latin translations. His knowledge of law is vouched by his abundant use of legal terms, evidence rather of his friendship with lawyers and his appetite for jargon. He knew medicine enough to be house physician at the Lyon Hôtel Dieu and personal physician in the suite of the Cardinal du Bellay. Certainly this is evidence, almost the only specific evidence, of his achievement in learning. But it should not imply that he was a scientist. At most he did not advance the narrow limits of the medicine current in his time. He was an acceptable practitioner in a period of prolonged ignorance.

But such generalizations are less suggestive than what has been laboriously pieced together of his very meager chronology. In 1530 he was matriculated in medicine at the University of Montpellier. In 1532 he was practicing medicine at Lyon and publishing the Latin letters of the Italian physician Manardi, the *Aphorisms* of Hippocrates, the fabricated Cuspidius, and his own *Pantagruel.* This in two years. Within the two years preceding 1530 it is suggested that he may have studied law at Poitiers and visited other universities. Even if the suggestion could be brought

---

[12] *Ibid.,* p. 140.
[13] *Ibid.,* pp. 115 seq.

to the dignity of an inference, what would it guarantee of learning? Except for a single undated letter from the priory of Ligugé, we have no documentation on Rabelais from 1521 to 1530. But if indeed he did study law at Poitiers and did visit other universities before he turned to medicine, or if he picked up some medicine on the way, then he was superficially experimenting toward versatility. The issue is sometimes dodged by calling him a humanist.[14] But though he had humanist friends, he was obviously not a classicist. Or again, his learning, because his allusions are astonishingly various, is called encyclopedic. As a compliment to learning, the adjective is dubious; but in another sense it is suggestive of his intellectual curiosity and his acute awareness of words. Knowing that there is much to be learned, as Dr. Johnson said, from the backs of books, he was alert to pick up a little of everything. He found that for his new readers bits of lore had the interest of news. While they liked his samples of learning and relished his satire on the pedantries of humanism, the humanists, seeing more in the joke, relished it none the less. It was gay, but also thoughtful, escape from the solemn Renaissance fictions of classicism. Rabelais already knew his readers well enough to carry them wine on both shoulders.

The insistent and various extravagance anticipated journalism in that it was the cultivation of style as advertisement. Besides perennial excitements of substance he uses dialect, slang, jargon, parody, oratory, not in ebullience, not in occasional outbreak, but in constant

[14] Plattard, p. 117.

parade of style. He is a sensationalist; his readers are to be shocked and amused. So he turned to the grotesque, and so he pursued it. He has no winsome persons; his satire has no indignation; his laughter, no sympathy. In this aspect a most suggestive contrast is offered by Cervantes. "Cervantes laughed Spain's chivalry away" is unjust because it is shallow. From the beginning and throughout, *Don Quixote* thrives on what Rabelais precludes, geniality. The grotesque of Cervantes is human enough to make us feel a certain social service beyond laughter in attacks on windmills; and his great achievement is the creation of a grotesque whom we come to love.

3. HISTORY

History straddles the fundamental division of composition into the forms of discussion or persuasion on the one hand and, on the other, those of story or play. For history is now one, now the other, and now both together. Earlier chronicles, more or less epic, hardly discuss at all; some recent histories are so bent on analysis as hardly to narrate at all; and some of the greater histories, ancient or modern, Thucydides, Tacitus, Macchiavelli, bring the two into effective combination. In any age this last is so difficult as to demand superior grasp. Livy, for instance, being generally content with narrative, hardly makes even his imaginary orations to troops expository. But Thucydides, narrating effectively, is no less concerned to instruct his readers in the issues. His "Expedition against Syracuse" thus became both tragedy and sermon.

(*a*) *Latin Histories*

The fifteenth century shows the advance of history beyond chronicle in the Latin of Leonardo Bruni, of Arezzo (1369–1444; *Leonardi Aretini historiarum florentini populi libri XII,* Florence, 1855–1860, 3 vols., ed. by Mancini, Leoni, and Tonietti, with the Italian translation of Donato Acciajuoli). Chronicles nevertheless persisted; for they still had, perhaps still have, the values realized by Herodotus. But Bruni undertook and fairly accomplished something more: "history, which in so many simultaneous events must keep the longer sequence, explain the causes of single facts, and bring out the interpretation" (I. 52). Not quite Thucydides or Tacitus, perhaps, he has clearly moved in their direction. His style is periodic in habit without often conforming strictly, humanistic without being laboriously imitative or diffuse, intelligently Ciceronian without being inhibited by Ciceronianism. The orations inserted after the fashion of Livy show, indeed, that he felt bound to such amplitude, variety, and classical allusion as should climb the high style; but they are neither frequent nor conventionally decorative, and some of them are both lively and urgent pleas. The following examples are typical.

Book III: Pope Gregory to the Florentines for peace through the restoration of the exiles; and the Florentine speech of refusal.

Book IV: Ianus Labella for insuring the republic against the pride of the nobles.

Book VI: Debate of the Perugian envoys with the Florentines.

Book VIII: The Florentine envoys to the Pope; the Pope's reply and Barbadoro's indignant rejoinder.

Book XII: The Milanese legates at Venice against the Florentines, and the Florentine reply.

Bruni puts orations oftenest into the mouths of envoys to develop issues which he has already summarized. Generally they are terser than the speeches of the fashionable dialogues; and sometimes, for he had often been an envoy himself, they are warm with actual debate. In this way his narrative is interpreted by exposition. Remaining narrative in plan, it indicates the animating considerations and interprets the outcome.

Book I, for instance, closes a summary of ancient history with a survey of Italian cities after the invasions, and Frederick II's fatal widening of the breach between Empire and Papacy. Book II shows Florence in full republican career thwarted by factions; Book IV, the creation of the *vexillifer justitiae* as a republican means of checking the selfish ambitions of the nobles. The increasing use of mercenaries shown in Book VII leads to chronic difficulties detailed later. The last three books present the war with Milan not only in its succession of events, but also as a single enterprise.

Finishing his first book in 1416, his sixth in 1429, Bruni solemnly presented nine books to the Signory in 1439, and lived to finish his long labor before 1444.

De bello italico adversos gothos gesto historia (1441), an amplification of the summary in the first book of his History of Florence, has less interpretation. The steady, concise narrative, with little comment, has sometimes too little salience. But to attentive reading the story of battle after battle, now victory, now defeat, gradually gives some grasp of the military operations to hold Italy for Justinian. The main figure is Belisarius. Except in occasional concrete description, this history is more like Caesar's, and is an experiment in that expository narrative later mastered by Macchiavelli. Belisarius is clearly exhibited not only as marvelous in military science, but as an intelligent organizer and administrator. When he feels himself let down by Justinian, and is approached by the Goths toward a joint kingdom, he will not commit himself to any disloyalty. His triumphal return to Justinian reports his intelligent discipline in Italy. Later his recall to Italy after other generals had meantime failed finds the task of reorganization hopeless in the disaffection of the imperial soldiers so long unpaid and ill led. With very little comment or review Belisarius emerges clearly from the narrative itself.

Bruni's histories are evidence of a sober earlier humanism immune to the extravagances of Ciceronianism and to that allusive display that led to dilation. They go about their business. Oratory is kept subsidiary to the story and the message. This tradition of Latin history continues in the *Scotorum historiae* (1526) of Hector Boece, and again in the *Rerum scoticarum historia* (1582) of George Buchanan. Both wrote Latin history seriously as European scholars. Buchanan, sometimes arid and partisan, was nationalist, indeed, only in his later years. Meantime he had taught for many years in France, had written Latin tragedies, and had been saluted by Joseph Scaliger as the foremost of Latin poets. History, then, kept alive among the humanists the medieval tradition of international

Latin. Its classicism, more restrained and more intelligent, less of style than of method, was the more valid imitation.

(b) Vernacular Histories

MORE

Sir Thomas More's study of Richard III (*The History of King Richard the Thirde . . . Writen by Master Thomas More . . . 1513,* ed. J. R. Lumby, Cambridge, 1883) shows these preoccupations in both Latin and English. Though it is unfinished, it is not fragmentary, nor merely descriptive; it is a thoroughgoing interpretation. All the more conspicuous, therefore, is its concrete vividness. Though judge and afterward pamphleteer, More cast this history as story. He makes us understand largely by making us see. Thus the Queen surrenders her son.

All this notwithstanding, here I deliuer him, and hys brother in him, to kepe into your handes, of whom I shall aske them both afore God and the world. Faithfull ye be, that wot I wel, and I know wel ye be wise. Power and strength to kepe him if you list neither lacke ye of yourself nor can lack helpe in this cause. And if ye cannot elsewhere, than may ye leue him here. But only one thing I beseche you, for the trust that his father put in you euer and for the trust that I put in you now, that as farre as ye thinke that I fere to muche, be ye wel ware that ye fere not as farre to little. And therewithall she said vnto the child: Farewel, my own swete sonne; God send you good keping; let him kis you ones yet ere ye goe, for God knoweth when we shal kis togither agayne. And therewith she kissed him and blessed him, turned her back and wept and went her way, leauing the childe weping as fast. When the lord Cardinal and these other lordes with him had receiued this yong duke, thei brought him into the sterrechamber, where the protectour toke him in his armes and kissed him with these wordes: Now welcome, my lord, euen with al my very hart. And he sayd in that of likelihod as he thought. Thereupon forthwith they brought him to the kynge his brother into the bishoppes palice at Powles, and from thence through the citie honorably into the Tower, out of which after that day they neuer came abrode (40).

The three pages devoted to the episode of Shore's wife, lively at once with irony and with image, pass to calm estimate and moral reflection.

And for thys cause as a goodly continent prince, clene and faultles of himself, sent out of heauen into this vicious world for the amendment of mens maners, he caused the bishop of London to put her to open penance, going before the crosse in procession upon a Sonday with a taper in her hand. In which she went in countenance and pace demure so womanly, and albeit she were out of al array saue her kyrtle only, yet went she so fair and louely, namelye while the wondering of the people caste a comly rud in her chekes, of whiche she before had most misse, that her great shame wan her much praise. . . . But me semeth the chaunce so much the more worthy to be remembred in how much she is now in the more beggerly condicion, vnfrended and worne out of acquaintance, after good substance, after as gret fauour with the prince, after as gret sute and seking to with al those that those days had busynes to spede, as many other men were in their times, which be now famouse only by the infamy of their il dedes. Her doinges were not much lesse, albeit thei be much lesse remembred because thei were not so euil (53).

The conversations of the Duke of Buckingham with Cardinal Morton, functioning as exposition, close at the end of More's manuscript almost as a scene in a play.

The duke laughed merely at the tale, and said: My lord, I warant you neither the lyon nor the bore shal pyke anye matter at any thyng here spoken; for it shall neuer come nere their eare. In good fayth, sir, said the bishop, if it did, the thing that I was about to say, taken as wel as afore God I ment it, could deserue but thank; and yet taken as I wene it wold, might happen to turne me to litle good and you to lesse. Then longed the duke yet moch more to wit what it was. Wherupon the byshop said: In good faith, my lord, as for the late protector, sith he is now king in possession, I purpose not to dispute his title. But for the weale of this realm, wherof his grace hath now the gouernance, and wherof I am my self one poore member, I was about to wish that to those habilities wherof he hath already right many litle nedyng my prayse, it might yet haue pleased God for the better store to haue geuen him some of suche other excellente vertues mete for the rule of a realm as our Lorde hath planted in the parsone of youre grace (91).

More's diction is discreetly popular, both choice and homely, pointed with proverbs, occasionally reminiscent of popular poetry.

The Quene her self satte alone alowe on the rishes all desolate and dismayde (20).

The management of sentences is less expert. More, as many other humanists, was bilingual to the extent of composing habitually in Latin even when he meant to publish in the vernacular. *Richard III* he composed in both. This may partly explain his frequent use of what are now subordinating conjunctions to begin sentences. *Wherefore* is often used in sixteenth-century English, as Latin *quare,* where modern use requires *therefore.* But when allowance is made for this, there still remains some uncertainty as to sentence boundaries, some doubt as to whether an added clause is subordinate or independent. Writing racy English for the larger audience, More tolerated the looser aggregative habit of English prose in his time. But his English, as well as his Latin, shows clear grasp of the period, and even occasional strict conformity. Current English still lagged in this respect throughout the century. Before Hooker English prose is generally less controlled than Italian. On the other hand, More uses balance and epigram discreetly, not for decorative display, but strictly for point; and his shifting from longer aggregations to sharp short sentences gives pleasant variety.

MACCHIAVELLI

Narrative and exposition are perfectly fused in Macchiavelli (*Istorie fiorentine, testo critico con introduzione e note per cura di Plinio Carli,* Florence, Sansoni, 1927, 2 vols.). His history of Florence (1532) not only has an insistent moral; it is at once narrative and expository. While we see the events, we see into them. His analytic narrative carries the orator's art of *narratio*,[15] the statement of the facts involved in an argument, to greater scope. We follow Macchiavelli not merely as assenting to his conclusions, but as reaching them ourselves. The more distinctively narrative values of vividness and directness he brings out often enough to show his control. But his ultimate object is not imaginative realization; it is rather persuasion. The sequence is not only of events, but of ideas. The admirable orations given to leaders at crises are not merely conventional, nor mainly to characterize

[15] For *narratio*, see ARP.

the speaker as a person in a play, but to expound the situation. Livian in model, they are oratory of a higher order, both acutely reasoned and persuasive.

Macchiavelli's exposition is sometimes separate, as in the essay that prefaces each book, or in those *sententiae* that from time to time open vistas of thought.

Beyond doubt rancor seems greater and strokes are heavier when liberty is recovered than when it is defended (II. xxxvii. 123).

For a republic no law can be framed which is more vicious than one that looks to the past (III. iii. 136).

No one who starts a revolution in a city should expect either to stop it where he intends, or to regulate it in his own way (III. x. 148).

Between men who aspire to the same position it is easy to arrange alliance, but not friendship (VI. ix. 34).

For men in power shame consists in losing, not in crooked winning (VI. xvii. 81).

Thereupon arose in the city those evils which oftenest spawn in a peace. For the young, freer than usual, spent immoderately on dress, suppers, and such luxuries, and being idle, wasted their time and substance on gaming and women. Their study was to appear splendid in dress, sage and astute in speech; and he who was quickest with biting phrase was wisest and most esteemed (VII. xxviii. 155).

Force and necessity, not written promises and obligations, make princes keep faith (VIII. xxii. 198).

But most of his exposition is not added; it is welded. The narrative itself is made expository by a constant chain of cause and effect. It is clear both in its events and in their significance for policy. We learn at every turn not only what Florence did, but why; and we forecast the result. Stefano Porcari, lamenting the decay of the Church

(VI. xxix. 101), is inspired by Petrarch's "Spirto gentil."
The account of the conspiracy nipped by the Pope is rather
a story plot than a story. Macchiavelli is content to suggest
that it was operatic. He is not concerned to work out its
story values; he is bent on its historical significance. The
spectacles at the wedding of Lorenzo to Clarice (VII. xxi.
148) are not elaborated descriptively; they are summed
up as indicative of the habit of the time. So is handled
(VII. xxxiii. 162) Professor Cola Montano's doctrinaire
enthusiasm for republics and scorn of tyrants. His pupils
find the issue in assassination. The splendid audience of
the Pope (VIII. xxxvi. 218) to the ambassadors of Florence for reconciliation is at once description and argument.
Thus the progress of the *Istorie fiorentine* is simultaneously of facts and of ideas. It is analyzed narrative.

Fused also is the style. Heightened for the orations
(II. xxxiv; III. v, xi, xiii, xxiii; IV. xxi; V. viii, xi, xxi,
xxiv; VI. xx; VII. xxiii; VIII. x), it is never decorated,
never diffused, so ascetically conformed to its message as
never to obtrude. This is not negatively the art that knows
how to conceal itself, but positively the art that is devoted
singly. True in the choice of words, it is expert in the
telling emphasis of sentences. Its reasoned balances suffice
without the empty iteration of English euphuism. They
are played never for display, always for point. The Latin
period, welcome to the habit of Macchiavelli's mind, is
rarely pushed to a conformity that would in the vernacular
have seemed artificial. Macchiavelli's sentences are in
logic fifty years ahead of the French and the English; but
they do not force his own vernacular.

Chapter IX

ESSAYS

1. DISCUSSIONS ON POLITICS AND SOCIETY

TWO Italian books of the early sixteenth century became so famous as to be almost proverbial. Written about the same time, Macchiavelli's *Principe* (1513) and Castiglione's *Cortegiano* (1514) are complementary. Macchiavelli expounds princely policy in war and in the truces between wars; Castiglione leads princely leisure into culture. The policy and the culture are parts of the same Italian world; but the two books are in sharpest contrast. Macchiavelli's facts are strictly analyzed; Castiglione's are habitually idealized. Macchiavelli's style is stripped and so fused with the message as to be inseparable; Castiglione's is ample, manipulating the decorative diffuseness of its time and its setting to elegance. Macchiavelli's economy is insistent, urgent; Castiglione's is gracious, deliberate, suggestive, rising to oratory. Both men used their thorough control of Latin to shape their writing of Italian prose; but Macchiavelli was applying rather such compression as that of Tacitus, Castiglione the composition of Cicero.

It is Macchiavelli's triumph that consideration of his doctrine has quite submerged his style.

I have not adorned nor distended this book with ample cadences, nor with precious or magnificent words or any other extrinsic charm or ornament, such as many are wont to use for descriptive decoration; for I have wished that nothing might win it praise, in other words that it should be acceptable only for the truth of its matter and the gravity of its subject (Dedication to Lorenzo).

Since my object is to write something useful to him who understands it, I have thought it more fitting to follow rather the effectual truth of the thing itself than its concept [immaginazione] (Opening of xv).

His name soon became a byword; for Englishmen and Frenchmen found it easier to denounce Italian statecraft than to explain wherein their own was different. Formulated for Italian despots, his doctrine that the safety and independence of the state are paramount over any consideration of justice or mercy became more and more sinister in terms of the rising new national monarchs beyond his ken. In the composition of the whole Macchiavelli was still young. He had not yet achieved the sure control felt in his *Istorie fiorentine*. Masterly already in expository analysis, eloquent in its close, the *Principe* has not a compelling logical sequence.

In sequence and in detail the *Cortegiano* is more mature than Macchiavelli's *Principe*. Castiglione kept it by him ten years. The final revision (Codex Laurentianus, Rome, 1524) was published at Florence in 1528. All this care left the diction unpretentious. Scholarly without pedantry, Castiglione even forestalls the Tuscans by openly proclaiming his right to Lombard words. "I have written in my own tongue, and as I speak, and to those who speak as I do." Thinking often of rhetoric, feeling the Latin period and attentive to *clausula,* he applies his lore to Italian sentences without stiffness or formality, happily reconciling gravity with ease. Encomium, inevitable in his subject and his time, is oftener implied than dilated. The plan of the dialogue is taken from Cicero's *De oratore.* Reminiscence in detail is negligible. Castiglione's imitation is not the common Renaissance borrowing of passages; it is the adaptation of Cicero's plan for presenting the typical Roman statesman to survey of the typical Italian. Thus the dialogue is Ciceronian in proceeding logically from point to point. Within the frame of Cicero the conduct of the book expands the dialogue toward conversation. This is not dramatic dialogue; nor is it imitation of the Platonic quest. Rather Castiglione's intention was to realize the human scene, to flavor the point with the speaker; and his achievement in suggesting the gracious interchange of the court of Urbino has been found quite as significant as the conclusions of his debates.

For the *Cortegiano* is one of the few Renaissance books that have endured the test of time. Details of place and time have been made to carry so much larger human suggestion that it has been reprinted again and again; it has been widely translated; it has today an audience not only of special students, but of the many more who love literature. Though the very term "courtier" is obsolete, though the particular social function soon faded, the book endures. It is not only the best of Renaissance dialogues; it is a classic.

The *Utopia* (1516) of Sir Thomas More, beginning as a dialogue on certain social evils in England, passes to descriptive exposition of a state organized and operated solely for the common weal. Though the name *Utopia* means "nowhere," this polity is described as the actual experience of a returned traveler. The literary form is thus reminiscent of Lucian, whom More ten years before had translated with Erasmus. It is reminiscent also of Plato, of the travelers' tales popular in that age of discovery and explanation, and more faintly of those distant or fortunate isles (*îles lointaines*) which had often been posed as abodes of idealized communities. But though these hints were doubtless intended, they are incidental. They fade as we read on.

Unfortunately for More's literary reputation, most of us read his best-known book only in a pedestrian translation (Ralph Robinson, 1551; second edition, 1556). Keeping much of the vivacity of the diction, this is quite unequal to More's flexible Latin rhythms.[1] For More, as for Poliziano and Leonardo Aretino, Erasmus and Buchanan, Latin was a primary language. But whereas Erasmus had, so to speak, no effective vernacular, More's literary achievement in English is both distinguished in itself and ahead of his time. In spite of some uncertain ascriptions, we may be fairly sure that the English version of his *Richard III*,[2] as well as the Latin, is his own.

---

[1] In the prefatory epistle to Petrus Aegidius about two-thirds of the first hundred clauses conform to the *cursus* of the curial *dictamen* (MRP). These clauses compose about twenty sentences ending: *planus*, 6 (30%); *tardus*, 2 (10%); *velox*, 7 (35%); unconformed, 5 (25%). Inconclusive, this may be worth further study.

[2] See above, Chapter VIII.

ESSAYS 227

Continued discussion of the prince and the state moved Sir Thomas Elyot (1490?–1546) to make an English compilation for the widening circle of readers, *The Governour* (1531, ed. H. S. Croft, London, 1883, 2 vols.). "I have nowe enterprised," he says in a proem to Henry VIII, "to describe in our vulgare tunge the fourme of a juste publike weale, whiche mater I have gathered as well of the sayenges of moste noble autours (grekes and latynes) as by myne owne experience." But the "governour" and the "juste publike weale" receive no consistent discussion.

The opening chapters, postulating *order,* proceed thence to *honour* (i.e., rank), and so to *one sovereign.* Their review of history is very slight; and from Chapter iv Book I is occupied rather with the education of a gentleman. Book II is composed mainly of *exempla* to illustrate the virtues appropriate to high position; and Book III adds little more than further classified aggregation.

With no further design, without even a distinct idea, *The Governour* has of course no logical progress. Lawyer and something of a diplomat, Elyot was not a thinker. Reading widely without discrimination, and sometimes apparently at second hand, he compiled under headings. His later *Bankette of Sapience* (second edition? 1542) is a collection of *sententiae* arranged alphabetically under abstinence, adversity, affection, ambition, authoritie, amitie, apparaile, almsdeede, accusation, arrogance, etc. His *Governour,* though its headings have more logic, is hardly consecutive. In sources as in topics the book is a miscellany.

I. vii, viii, for instance, on a gentlemanly, not a professional knowledge of music, painting, and sculpture, suggest the *Cortegiano;* xii inquires "why gentilmen in this present time be not equal in doctryne to the auncient noblemen"; xiv proposes *exempla* for law students. After finding England deficient in the fine arts (140), he returns to law students with a recommendation of rhetoric, and thereupon itemizes it (149) under *status, inventio,* etc. By the end of the book he has passed from prudence to chess, archery, tennis, and bowls.

Elyot's diction, though he wishes to "augment our Englysshe tongue," is Latinized sparingly. *Copie* in the sense of the Latin *copia,* was fairly common in his time. He adds, e.g., *allecte* and *allectyve, coarted, fatigate, fucate, illecebrous, infuded, propise,* and *provecte.* His generally unpretentious habit is sometimes concretely racy.

Jean Bodin's treatise on historical method (*Methodus ad facilem historiarum cognitionem,* 1566),[3] giving high praise to Guicciardini, differs from him in conception. For Bodin, history is less a progress in time than a thesaurus of *exempla.*

Dividing it into human, natural, and divine, he would have us begin with a chronological reference table (ii), proceed to a more detailed survey, such as Funck's or Melanchthon's, advance to the histories of particular nations, Jews, Greeks, Romans, and then to such smaller communities as Rhodes, Venice, and Sicily, with constant attention to geography.

In iii, *De locis historiarum recte instituendis,* the topics are first the commonplaces of encomium: birth, endowments,

[3] Citations are from Jacobus Stoer's edition of 1595.

achievements, morals, culture. From the family, which for Bodin is the starting point of history, we are to proceed to the organization of the state and the developments of the arts.

De historicorum delectu (iv) has many specific and acute estimates of both ancients and moderns. "Somehow those who are active in wars and affairs (44) shy at writing; and those who have given themselves somewhat more to literature are so possessed with its charms and sweetness as hardly to think in other terms." Bodin himself is broad enough to praise both Plutarch and Tacitus.

De recto historiarum iudicio (v), beginning with geography, proceeds to regional traits. The approach is suggestive; but the development is little more than aggregation under those dubious headings Northern and Southern, Eastern and Western.

At this point (vi) Bodin begins the analysis of the state: the elemental family, the citizen, the magistrate, the king. "Macchiavelli, indeed, the first after some twelve hundred years since the barbarians to write on the state, has won general currency; but there is no doubt that he would have written several things more truly and better if he had added legal tradition (*usus*) to his knowledge of ancient philosophers and historians" (140). Monarchy is found to be the ideal form of government. The golden age of primitive peace and happiness is proved to be a senile fancy (vii). Let us rather, relying on the science of numbers, *De temporis universi ratione* (viii), compute the recurrence of historical "cycles." Strange conclusion to so much hard reasoning!

Systematically analytical, the book is easier to consult than to follow; but its Latin style is of that sincere, capable, unpretentious sort which had been established for history by the Italians. The political ideas of the *Methodus* are carried out by the same systematic analysis in Bodin's second book, *Les Six Livres de la république,* 1576.[4] Greek and Latin political usage is made by a long wall of citations to support, with other proofs from history, the theory of absolute monarchy.

Such support of the new monarchies by a reasoned theory based on ancient history·did not pass unchallenged. George Buchanan, with more literary competence in Latin, though with less knowledge of politics, offered for his little Scotland a theory of monarchy answerable to the people (*De jure regni apud Scotos dialogus,* 1579).[5] The preface, addressed to James VI, keeps a tutorial tone, as of one still laying down the law. The occasion put forth for the Ciceronian dialogue is French reprobation of Scotch politics. How shall this be met? The method is evident from the first three points.

To distinguish a king from a tyrant, we must remember that society is founded not only on utility, but on natural law implanted by God. A king is typically shepherd, leader, governor, physician, created not for his own ends, but for the welfare of his people (1–6).

Kingship, being an *ars* based on *prudentia,* needs guidance by laws (8). Objection: who would be king on these terms? Answer: ancient history and doctrine show motives higher than lust for power and wealth (9).

These two points being iterated in summary for transition, the third is the need not only of laws, but of a council (11–14).

[4] The fourth edition, cited here, by Gabriel Cartier, 1599. Meantime Bodin had published in 1586 a revised edition in Latin, *De re publica libri vi.*

[5] Edition cited Edinburgh (Freebairn), 1715, *Opera omnia,* ed. Thomas Ruddiman, Vol. I.

The many *exempla* from ancient and modern history confirming or challenging the *a priori* progress of the dialogue do not touch the recent events that raised the question. Scotch history is used even less specifically than ancient to confirm the theory of limited monarchy. But though Buchanan does not prove that recent politics were an application of his theory, he makes the theory itself interesting and sometimes persuasive.

The Latin style has more liveliness, expertness, and range than Bodin's. But the argument, though urgent as well as scholastically ingenious, remains unconvincing. After debating general considerations inconclusively, it falls back at last on the particular customs and needs of Scotland. These are not applied specifically enough to be determining. The expertness of the dialogue is rather literary than argumentative.

Brought down to the market place by printing, controversy by the end of the century was learning the ways of journalism in pamphlets. Meantime printing had opened such compilation as Elyot's, samples of learning for those eager readers who had not gone to school with the Latin manuals of Erasmus.

The best of these sixteenth-century discussions, the piercing urgency of Macchiavelli, the charming exposition of Castiglione, the philosophical survey of More, the systematic analysis of Bodin, the hot attack of Buchanan, are all essays in that modern sense of the word which applies it to consecutive exposition involving argument. They show essay-writing of this kind—which was to move more surely in the seventeenth century—already on a firm footing. They recognize the Italian tradition of history in abjuring the decorative dilation which was habitual in other fields. They show Latin and vernacular side by side, and vernacular prose gaining point and finish from the Latin commanded by all their writers. They are a solid literary achievement of the Renaissance.

2 . MONTAIGNE

The other kind of essay, the literary form that has kept the original meaning of attempt, sketch, experiment, had its pace set late in the sixteenth century by Montaigne. Nothing could be farther removed than his habit from tidy system or consecutive argument. Devoted to the reading of history, and eager to share its profits, he had no mind to follow the Italian tradition of writing history. *Essai* in his practice is not the settling of a subject, but the trying. He makes one approach, then another, suggesting relations that he does not carry out. With many *exempla* he invites us to accumulate philosophy of living. If we do not coöperate, if we do not think them over, his essays remain collections of items in memorable phrase, without compelling sequence of ideas. For Montaigne is not the kind of philosopher who integrates a system; he is a sage. He has the sage's oral habit. No writing conveys more the impression of thinking aloud. Again and again he writes as if making up his mind, not before utterance, but by the very process of utterance. Macchiavelli, or Bodin, having made up his mind fully and finally, tries to convince us; Montaigne, as if making up his in our company, throws out suggestions.

True, some few of his essays are more consecutive developments of what he has concluded. His early and widely quoted *Education of Children* (II. xxvi) has even some logical progress.

But logical sequence is not Montaigne's habit. His many revisions[6] show him leaning more and more on the aggregation of separate suggestions. He changes words, he adds instances, but he does not seek a stricter order.

> But I am going off a little to the left of my theme. . . . I, who take more pains with the weight and usefulness of my discourses than with their order and sequence, need not fear to lodge here, a little off the track, a fine story (II. xxvii).

> This bundling of so many various pieces is made on condition that I put hand to it only when urged by too lax a leisure, and only when I am at home (II. xxxvii, opening).

His usual lack of sequence, then, is not careless. The careless fumbling that comes from muddled thinking he ridicules.

> They themselves do not yet know what they mean, and you see them stammer in bringing it forth, and judge that their labor is not in childbirth, but in conception, and that they are only licking what is not yet formed (I. xxvi).

As to sequence he even catechizes himself.

> Is it not making bricks without straw, or very like, to build books without science and without art? The fantasies of music are conducted by art, mine by chance.

And his answer is very earnest.

> At least I have this from my course of study (*discipline*), that never a man treated a subject that he understood and

[6] See F. Strowski, *Montaigne* (Paris, 1931).

knew better than I do the one that I have undertaken, and that in this subject I am the most learned man alive; secondly, that no one ever penetrated farther into its material, nor peeled more sedulously its parts and their consequences, nor reached more precisely and fully the end that he had proposed for his job. To accomplish this, I need bring no more than fidelity. That I have, the most sincere and pure that is to be found (III. ii).

Montaigne's method, then, is deliberate.[7] If he passes, as in *Des coches* (III. vi), from examples of lavish display to the cruelty of Spanish conquest in Mexico and frankly begins his last paragraph with *retumbons à nos coches,* that is because he usually prefers to take us on a journey around his idea. Hundreds of readers have found the talk of such a guide on the way more winsome than the conclusions of others after they have come home.

The art of growing an idea by successive additions sets the pace also for his sentences. Knowing Latin, he tells us, as a native language, and better than French, he puts aside Cicero for Seneca. This is more than the rejection of Ciceronianism, more than preference for Seneca's philosophy; it is in detail the same aggregative method that he uses for the composition of a whole essay. That vernacular sentences were commonly more aggregative than those of Augustan Latin may have been a reason for his choosing the vernacular. At any rate, he keeps the two languages quite apart. Instead of applying his Latin to

[7] "Qu'il n'est rien si contraire à mon style qu'une narration estendue (i.e., *narratio,* sustained exposition) ; je me recouppe si souvent à fault d'haleine; je n'ay ni composition ny explication qui vaille" (I. xxi).

the pointing of his French sentences, he prefers to let them accumulate as in talk.

(1) They do still worse who keep the revelation of some intention of hatred toward their neighbor for their last will,
(2) having hid it during their lives,
(3) and show that they care little for their own honor,
(4) irritating the offense by bringing it to mind,
(5) instead of bringing it to conscience,
(6) not knowing how, even in view of death, to let their grudge die,
(7) and extending its life beyond their own. (I. vii.)

The sentence might easily have been recast in a Latin period; Montaigne prefers to let it reach its climax by accumulation.

(1) Nature has furnished us, as with feet for walking, so with foresight to guide our lives,
(2) foresight not so ingenious, robust, and pretentious as the sort that explores (*invention*),
(3) but as things come, easy, quiet, and healthful,
(4) and doing very well what other people say,
(5) in those who have the knack of using it simply and regularly,
(6) that is to say, naturally. (III. xiii.)

So his epigrams are comparatively few and simple. His many memorable sayings are not paraded as *sententiae*.

It is not a soul, not a body, that we are educating; it is a man (I. xxvi).

Unable to regulate events, I regulate myself, and adjust myself to them if they do not adjust themselves to me (II. xvii).

The teaching that could not reach their souls has stayed on their lips (III. iii).

Between ourselves, two things have always seemed to me in singular accord, supercelestial opinions and subterranean morals (III. xiii).

For Montaigne's shrewd summaries prevail less often by balanced sentences than by concrete diction.

I am seldom seized by these violent passions. My sensibility is naturally dense; and I encrust and thicken it daily by discourse (I. ii).

Anybody's job is worth sounding; a cowherd's, a mason's, a passer-by's, all should be turned to use, and each lend its wares; for everything comes handy in the kitchen (I. xxvi).

Such sentences, such diction, are not only his practice; they are part of his literary theory.

The speech that I like is simple and direct, the same on paper as on the lips, speech succulent and prompt (*nerveux*), curt and compact, not so much delicate and smoothed as vehement and brusque—*Haec demum sapiet dictio quae feriet*—rather tough than tiresome, shunning affectation, irregular, loose, and bold, each bit for itself, not pedantic, not scholastic, not legal, but rather soldierly (I. xxvi).

The urgent metrical sentence of poetry seems to me to soar far more suddenly and strike with a sharper shock [The figure is of a falcon] (I. xxvi).

These good people (Vergil and Lucretius) had no need of keen and subtle antitheses. Their diction is all full, and big with a natural and constant force. They are all epigram, not only the tail, but the head, the stomach, and the feet. . . . It is an eloquence not merely soft and faultless; it is prompt and firm, not so much pleasing as filling and quickening the strongest minds. When I see those brave forms of expression, so vivid, so deep, I do not call it good speaking; I call it good thinking (III. v).[8]

[8] This is the doctrine of Quintilian, whom he quotes. ARP.

So he cannot stomach that Renaissance imitation which ran to borrowing, nor that display of Latin style for itself which published even private letters.

Those indiscreet writers of our century who go sowing in their worthless works whole passages from the ancients to honor themselves (I. xxvi).

But it surpasses all baseness of heart in persons of their rank that they have sought to derive a principal part of their fame from chatter and gossip, even to using the private letters written to their friends (I. xl).

So he is impatient with the unreality of romance.

Going to war only after having announced it, and often after having assigned the hour and place of battle (I. v).

Those Lancelots, Amadis, Huons, and such clutter of books to amuse children (I. xxvi).

Reviewing contemporary criticism of poetry, he says: "We have more poets than judges and interpreters of poetry; it is easier to make it than to know it" (I. xxxvii). "You may make a fool of yourself anywhere else," he warns, "but not in poetry" (II. xvii). So there is no room for mediocre poetry.

Popular, purely natural poetry has simplicities and graces comparable with the eminent beauty of poetry artistically perfect, as is evident in the Gascon villanelles and in songs brought to us from illiterate peoples. Mediocre poetry, which is neither the one nor the other, is disdained, without honor or even esteem (I. liv).

Dismissing in a scornful phrase "the Spanish and Petrarchist fanciful elevations" (II. x), he exactly estimates the Latin poets of his time as "good artisans in that

craft" (II. xvii). Perhaps a certain significance, therefore, attaches to his repeating the current complacency
with regard to French poetry.

I think it has been raised to the highest degree it will ever
attain; and in those directions in which Ronsard and Du
Bellay excel I find them hardly below the ancient perfection
(II. xvii).

Elsewhere, and habitually, Montaigne's attitude toward
the classics was quite different from the habit of the
Renaissance. He sought not so much the Augustans as
Seneca and the Plutarch of Amyot.

Je n'ay dressé commerce avec aucun livre solide sinon Plu-
tarque et Seneque, où je puyse comme les Danaides, remplis-
sant et versant sans cesse (I. xxvi).

These, and even Cicero and Vergil, he sought not for
style, but for philosophy and morals. That sounder
classicism of composition which, through the Italian
tradition of history, had animated Renaissance essayists
of the stricter sort he put aside. He was not interested in
the ancient rhetoric of composition, nor, to judge from
his slight attention to it, in that field of ancient poetic.
He quotes both Dante and Tasso, but not in that aspect.
He is not interested in the growing appreciation of
Aristotle's *Poetic*. In this disregard of composition, indeed, he was of the Renaissance; but he rejected and even
repudiated Renaissance pursuit of classicism in style.
There he adopted the sound doctrine of Quintilian and
scornfully, to use his own word, abjured borrowed plumes
and decorative dilation. If we use the word classical in

its typical Renaissance connotation, we must call Montaigne, as well as Rabelais, anti-classical. Unlike as they are otherwise, they agree in satirizing Renaissance classicism.

The positive aspect of this rejection is Montaigne's homely concreteness. Trying to teach his readers, not to dazzle them, he is very carefully specific. To leave no doubt of his meaning, he will have it not merely accepted, but felt. Therefore he is more than specific; he is concrete. Imagery for him is not mythology; it is of native vintage.

"In this last scene between death and us there is no more pretending. We have to speak French; we have to show how much that is good and clean is left at the bottom of the pot" (I. xix). Such expression strikes us not as wit, not as an aristocrat's catering to the new public, but as the sincere use of sensory terms to animate ideas. If it reminds us sometimes of popular preaching, that is because Montaigne was a sage.

INDEX